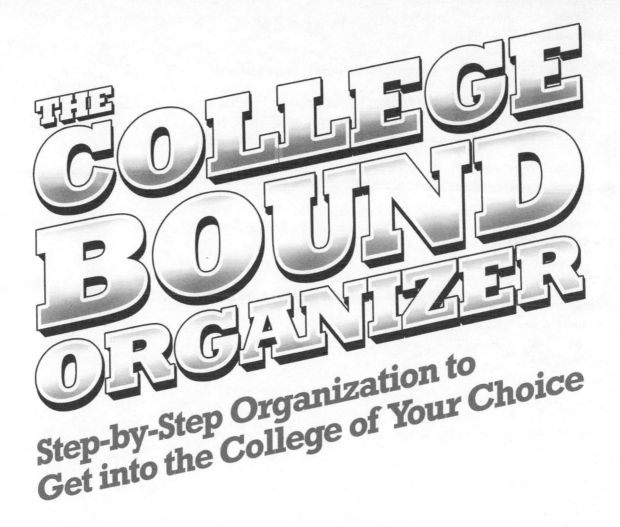

THE COLLEGE BOUND ORGANIZER

Step-by-Step Organization to Get into the College of Your Choice

ANNA COSTARAS AND GAIL LISS

Foreword by Edward B. Fiske

author of **Fiske Guide to Colleges**

sourcebooks **edu**

Published by Sourcebooks, Inc.
P.O. Box 4410, Naperville, Illinois 60567-4410
(630) 961-3900
Fax: (630) 961-2168
www.sourcebooks.com

Library of Congress Cataloging-in-Publication Data

Costaras, Anna.
 The college bound organizer / Anna Costaras and Gail Liss ; foreword by Edward B. Fiske.
     p. cm.
1. College student orientation--United States--Handbooks, manuals, etc. 2. Universities and colleges--Admission--Handbooks, manuals, etc. I. Liss, Gail. II. Title.
 LB2343.32.C67 2013
 378.1'98--dc23

                              2012029762

          Printed and bound in the United States of America.
              VP 10 9 8 7 6 5 4 3 2 1

Emmy, Jessica, and Alix
and
James, Christopher, and Michael

Thank you for leading us down this unexpected path.

CONTENTS

FOREWORD

There are more than 2,200 four-year colleges in the United States, and trying to figure out which ones are likely to be good matches for *you* can seem like a daunting task. It's easy to sympathize with the applicant to Haverford College some years ago who was particularly stressed out at the end of his on-campus interview. On his way back to the waiting room he had to pass through several doors, but his emotional state was such that he failed to notice where he was and opened one more door—which took him into a closet. He was so embarrassed that he remained in the closet for several minutes before reappearing to face a room full of staring faces.

It doesn't have to be that way.

As author of the *Fiske Guide to Colleges* and numerous other books on college admissions, I've had the pleasure of working with thousands of college-bound high school students and their parents both in person and through my writing. People are not born brain-wired knowing how to navigate the byzantine admissions process that American colleges and universities have in their wisdom imposed on their aspiring students, so a bit of anxiety—or at least mild bewilderment—is probably a sign that you are in touch with reality.

Not surprisingly, the most common question that I have gotten over the years from students staring at all those options is: Where do I start? The implicit subtext is: How do I begin to make sense of the process? My usual (and admittedly self-serving) suggestion is to thumb through the 300+ narrative descriptions in the *Fiske Guide* and find one or two schools that seem like a good match. Then look at the schools with which these schools have substantial overlapping applicant pools and maybe look at overlaps of the overlaps. This process should produce a list of 15 or 20 target schools to get you off and running.

Once you have identified some target schools, the challenge is to figure out how to deal with all the elements that go into the application process: campus visits, test-taking, financial aid forms, letters of reference, and so forth. That, of course, is where *The College Bound Organizer* comes to your rescue in at least two ways. First, it gives you a "one-stop shopping" way to keep track of the hundreds of details that go into applying to multiple colleges. No more ruffling through piles of papers to figure out when—or even whether!—you have scheduled an appointment with the admissions folks at Old Siwash. Second, it represents a checklist—with deadlines—that lays out the various steps that you need to be taking. With *The College Bound Organizer* at your side, you can rest assured that you will not wake up on December 31 and suddenly realize that you forgot to ask your English teacher for a recommendation that is due two days later.

Applying to college should be a positive experience. Colleges are interesting places, with lots of bright people doing innovative things, and the application process is really the beginning of your college education. It's the time when you begin to think seriously about your goals and academic interests. The mechanics of the process are important and need to be taken seriously. But it's also important to keep your mind on the big picture: which are the colleges that are best suited to help you to grow academically, socially, spiritually, and in every other way? Using *The College Bound Organizer* is one way to help you stay focused on what is really important.

Edward B. Fiske
Author of Fiske Guide to Colleges

INTRODUCTION

Congratulations, you're about to get started on an exciting adventure! Going to college is an amazing time in your life. There is much to look forward to: meeting your roommate, setting up your dorm room, attending sporting events, being independent, making new friends, and, of course, learning so many new things. You'll have exciting choices to make, from courses, to focus of study and professors to learn from. But first, you have to get there.

Welcome to *The College Bound Organizer*.

Organization is key to minimizing your (and your parents') stress and anxiety when applying to college. Organizing the college search and application process is essential because you also need to stay focused on academics, athletics, extracurricular commitments, jobs, family—all the interests, obligations, and activities that fill your day.

What do you need to organize? All the information and paperwork necessary to:

- COMPILE your personal profile
- SUBMIT your standardized test scores
- RESEARCH schools to identify your best fit
- COMPLETE your applications on time
- REVIEW your choices
- COMMIT to your school

You'll begin by defining who you are: your academic experience, extracurricular activities, athletics, community service, as well as relevant work and summer activities. Include recognition and awards. It took you years to accomplish all this, and you now have a few months to accurately and positively reflect on who you are and communicate this message. *The College Bound Organizer* helps you list, sort, and polish your accomplishments so they're ready to be reviewed by the admissions committees.

Soon, if not already, you'll be immersed in the standardized testing process. This guide includes sections for tracking test dates and locations, and recording scores to more easily help you decide which to submit.

Exploring your college and university options is the fun part of the application process. List possible choices and then become better acquainted with your options.

Whether you visit, search online, and/or meet with representatives on or off campus, jot down your impressions in the section provided. It is also important to keep track of your correspondence and communications with representatives.

Seeking financial aid may seem daunting. First, you'll need to understand the task at hand. Online resources, school guidance counselors, and college financial aid officers offer a wealth of information to help you get started. Completing forms accurately and submitting them on time can increase your chances of securing the aid you require.

Finally, you're ready to apply!

You'll be instructed how to set up file folders, one for each school you apply to and three to hold miscellaneous application and financial aid materials. Your folders will include the Bound to Organize worksheets you've completed, information you have collected, and application materials you have created for each specific school

Our system keeps you organized and focused along the way. You now hold everything you need to manage the massive amount of information you will be responsible for creating, requesting, and submitting, while meeting different deadlines for your applications.

Let's get started!

Anna and Gail

THINGS YOU'LL NEED TO GET STARTED

SHOPPING LIST

✓ 13 letter-size folders (label one folder "GENERAL" and set aside the rest until later)

✓ Large box for storage—wide enough to hold letter-size folders, documents, brochures, and catalogs

✓ Data storage device for document back-up

✓ 2" x 4" mailing labels (optional)

✓ 1" x 2⁵⁄₈" address labels (optional)

AND, DON'T FORGET

✓ One envelope to hold business cards you collect from admissions reps, college fairs, info sessions, interviews, etc.

✓ One envelope to collect delivery confirmation receipts for any materials you send to college admissions offices

Keep these two envelopes in your GENERAL folder.

CHAPTER 1

FACT FINDING: ALL ABOUT YOU!

In this section, you will store all of the information and facts about yourself, your family, and your high school that you will need to have at hand throughout the application process. You'll be required to provide all this information countless times when registering for tests and completing your applications, so easy access to this information will help you avoid endless aggravation. Having this information organized in one place will also minimize the chance of errors.

> **"One way to stay organized is to keep a list of the schools you applied to next to your computer with each school's user name and password. The user name and password always vary based on school, and it is best to be able to easily access this information. Students often become frustrated when they forget this information, and that only delays this process."**
>
> –REBECCA GOTTESMAN, Assistant Principal, Locust Valley High School, Locust Valley, New York

Start with your most basic personal information, such as your social security number and email address.

> **"Think about what your email address may or may not say about you."**
>
> –ALISON ALMASIAN, Director of Admissions,
> St. Lawrence University

If your email address reflects some funny nickname or private joke you have with your friends, get a new one! Set up a new address that is appropriate and easy to read. This is part of the identity you present to admissions officers.

Next, if you have not already done so, register with College Board and ACT in order to sign up for standardized tests including the SAT, SAT Subject Tests, and ACT. Record your user name and passwords for easy reference on the **Student's Personal Information** form.

Registering for standardized tests requires you to know your high school's SAT and ACT codes. In addition, your high school contact information will be required when you complete the Common Application and the Universal College Application (UCA), online undergraduate applications used by many colleges and universities. This same information is also needed for schools that require supplements to the Common App/UCA as well as schools that only accept their own applications. Spare yourself repeated searches by looking up this information once and recording it in the designated space.

Your family's education history is required information for both the Common App/UCA as well as many individual school applications. Later, when you begin applying to schools, you will need to collect information from family members about their education history.

My son had to call my alma mater to confirm my undergraduate completion date.

Completing the **Family Education Information** form in advance, along with the other forms in this chapter, will allow you to fill out your applications easily and with less chance for errors.

Financial aid information, including the FAFSA and CSS/Financial Aid PROFILE user names, passwords, and PINs, will not be needed until later in the process. Write this information on the **Student's Personal Information** form at the appropriate time.

Student's Personal Information

Social Security Number: _____

Email:_____

COLLEGE BOARD   www.collegeboard.com

User Name_____ Password_____

ACT   www.actstudent.org

User Name_____ Password_____

COMMON APPLICATION   www.commonapp.com

User Name_____ Password_____

UNIVERSAL COLLEGE APPLICATION   www.universalcollegeapp.com

User Name_____ Password_____

FAFSA   www.fafsa.ed.gov

Student PIN_____ Parent PIN_____

CSS/PROFILE   www.collegeboard.com

User Name_____ College Board Password_____

FASTWEB SCHOLARSHIPS   www.fastweb.com

User Name_____ Password_____

Family Education Information

MOTHER

Undergraduate School_____

Degree/Date of Graduation_____

Graduate School_____

Degree/Date of Graduation_____

Graduate School_____

Degree/Date of Graduation_____

FATHER

Undergraduate School_____

Degree/Date of Graduation_____

Graduate School_____

Degree/Date of Graduation_____

Graduate School_____

Degree/Date of Graduation_____

SIBLING _____

Undergraduate School_____

Degree/Date of Graduation_____

SIBLING _____

Undergraduate School_____

Degree/Date of Graduation_____

SIBLING _____

Undergraduate School_____

Degree/Date of Graduation_____

High School Information

School Name_____

Address_____

_____

SAT Code_____

ACT Code_____

Guidance/College Counselor Name_____

Telephone_____

Email_____

Fax_____

Additional Contact Name_____

Telephone_____

Email_____

Fax_____

CHAPTER 2

A SNAPSHOT OF YOUR HIGH SCHOOL YEARS: WHO ARE YOU?

You are a unique individual!

Your resume is the one place where you can demonstrate who you are. You'll list your passions, accomplishments, and the breadth and depth to which you've explored your interests. This is your opportunity to define yourself to the admissions committees.

"Students should consider highlighting the things into which they have poured the most time and effort, finding the things that have meant the most to them and the things in which they have made the greatest impact. Students need to understand that college admissions officers are trying to get a sense of the individual by evaluating how that individual has spent his or her time."

–PAUL W. HORGAN, Director of College Counseling, Cape Henry Collegiate School, Virginia Beach, Virginia

"Representing all that you do beyond academics with authenticity is very important."

–DARRYL W. JONES, Senior Associate Director of Admissions, Gettysburg College

"Both colleges and students have a duty to communicate who they are as effectively as possible to ensure the best possible matches."

–ALISON ALMASIAN, Director of Admissions, St. Lawrence University

This chapter provides seven *Who Are You?* worksheets. Identify the ones that apply to you and gather the information necessary to compile a complete and accurate profile of your high school years. The completed worksheets will enable you to easily fill out the activities section of the Common Application/UCA. You'll also be able to create a resume to submit either as a supplement to the Common App/UCA or with your applications to schools that don't use the Common App/UCA. Your resume can also be used when you apply for internships and jobs. Although you'll find some of the activity categories overlap, list your activities on the worksheet you think most fitting.

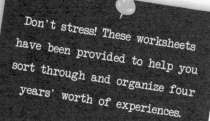

Don't stress! These worksheets have been provided to help you sort through and organize four years' worth of experiences.

- **Clubs/Extracurricular Activities** worksheet: include activities such as academic and social clubs, student newspaper, yearbook, music, theater/drama, culture and art, both in and outside of school. Don't forget to include leadership positions in any relevant activities.

- **Sports** worksheet: list all your teams, tournaments, and awards for athletic involvement in school-sponsored and independently run leagues. Highlight your leadership roles.

- **Community Service** worksheet: list your service involvement, both school sponsored and independent.

- **Awards** worksheet: explain all the academic achievements and non-academic distinctions you've earned throughout your high school years.

- **Competitions** worksheet: describe any contests in which you participated or are currently involved. These may include, but are not limited to, science, math, or engineering projects, writing submissions, art exhibitions, and debates.

- **Work Experience** worksheet: list paid and unpaid jobs and internships.

- **Summer Experiences** worksheet: list summer activities including travel, academic programs, athletic programs, and community outreach.

You can offer to share your resume with your recommenders to help brush them up on your accomplishments. Get your worksheets done early!

Most college applications require two recommendations in support of your file. While you're busy highlighting your accomplishments for your resume, this is the time to ask teachers, coaches, and others to write recommendations on your behalf. Once you have made these requests, complete the **Letters of Recommendation** log included in the back of this chapter.

Clubs/Extracurricular Activities

FRESHMAN YEAR

Name:	Dates:
Description:	
Position:	

Name:	Dates:
Description:	
Position:	

Name:	Dates:
Description:	
Position:	

Name:	Dates:
Description:	
Position:	

Name:	Dates:
Description:	
Position:	

Clubs/Extracurricular Activities

SOPHOMORE YEAR

Name:	Dates:
Description:	
Position:	

Name:	Dates:
Description:	
Position:	

Name:	Dates:
Description:	
Position:	

Name:	Dates:
Description:	
Position:	

Name:	Dates:
Description:	
Position:	

Clubs/Extracurricular Activities

JUNIOR YEAR

Name:	Dates:
Description:	
Position:	

Name:	Dates:
Description:	
Position:	

Name:	Dates:
Description:	
Position:	

Name:	Dates:
Description:	
Position:	

Name:	Dates:
Description:	
Position:	

Clubs/Extracurricular Activities

SENIOR YEAR

Name: Dates:

Description:

Position:

Name: Dates:

Description:

Position:

Name: Dates:

Description:

Position:

Name: Dates:

Description:

Position:

Name: Dates:

Description:

Position:

Sports

FRESHMAN YEAR

SPORT 1:	
Team 1:	Position:
Team 2:	Position:
Team 3:	Position:

SPORT 2:	
Team 1:	Position:
Team 2:	Position:
Team 3:	Position:

SPORT 3:	
Team 1:	Position:
Team 2:	Position:
Team 3:	Position:

Sports

SOPHOMORE YEAR

SPORT 1:	
Team 1:	Position:
Team 2:	Position:
Team 3:	Position:

SPORT 2:	
Team 1:	Position:
Team 2:	Position:
Team 3:	Position:

SPORT 3:	
Team 1:	Position:
Team 2:	Position:
Team 3:	Position:

Sports

JUNIOR YEAR

SPORT 1:	
Team 1:	Position:
Team 2:	Position:
Team 3:	Position:

SPORT 2:	
Team 1:	Position:
Team 2:	Position:
Team 3:	Position:

SPORT 3:	
Team 1:	Position:
Team 2:	Position:
Team 3:	Position:

Sports

SENIOR YEAR

SPORT 1:	
Team 1:	Position:
Team 2:	Position:
Team 3:	Position:

SPORT 2:	
Team 1:	Position:
Team 2:	Position:
Team 3:	Position:

SPORT 3:	
Team 1:	Position:
Team 2:	Position:
Team 3:	Position:

Community Service

FRESHMAN YEAR

Name of Organization:
Description of Role:
Dates:

Name of Organization:
Description of Role:
Dates:

Name of Organization:
Description of Role:
Dates:

Name of Organization:
Description of Role:
Dates:

Name of Organization:
Description of Role:
Dates:

Community Service

SOPHOMORE YEAR

Name of Organization:

Description of Role:

Dates:

Name of Organization:

Description of Role:

Dates:

Name of Organization:

Description of Role:

Dates:

Name of Organization:

Description of Role:

Dates:

Name of Organization:

Description of Role:

Dates:

Community Service

JUNIOR YEAR

Name of Organization:

Description of Role:

Dates:

Name of Organization:

Description of Role:

Dates:

Name of Organization:

Description of Role:

Dates:

Name of Organization:

Description of Role:

Dates:

Name of Organization:

Description of Role:

Dates:

Community Service

SENIOR YEAR

Name of Organization:

Description of Role:

Dates:

Name of Organization:

Description of Role:

Dates:

Name of Organization:

Description of Role:

Dates:

Name of Organization:

Description of Role:

Dates:

Name of Organization:

Description of Role:

Dates:

Awards

FRESHMAN YEAR

NAME OF AWARD	DATE

SOPHOMORE YEAR

NAME OF AWARD	DATE

JUNIOR YEAR

NAME OF AWARD	DATE

SENIOR YEAR

NAME OF AWARD	DATE

Competitions

FRESHMAN YEAR

Competition:

Project:

Date:

Outcome:

Competition:

Project:

Date:

Outcome:

Competition:

Project:

Date:

Outcome:

Competition:

Project:

Date:

Outcome:

Competition:

Project:

Date:

Outcome:

Competitions

SOPHOMORE YEAR

Competition:
Project:
Date:
Outcome:

Competition:
Project:
Date:
Outcome:

Competition:
Project:
Date:
Outcome:

Competition:
Project:
Date:
Outcome:

Competition:
Project:
Date:
Outcome:

Competitions

JUNIOR YEAR

Competition:
Project:
Date:
Outcome:

Competition:
Project:
Date:
Outcome:

Competition:
Project:
Date:
Outcome:

Competition:
Project:
Date:
Outcome:

Competition:
Project:
Date:
Outcome:

Competitions

SENIOR YEAR

Competition:
Project:
Date:
Outcome:

Competition:
Project:
Date:
Outcome:

Competition:
Project:
Date:
Outcome:

Competition:
Project:
Date:
Outcome:

Competition:
Project:
Date:
Outcome:

Work Experience

FRESHMAN YEAR

Employer:

Job Description:

Dates:

SOPHOMORE YEAR

Employer:

Job Description:

Dates:

JUNIOR YEAR

Employer:

Job Description:

Dates:

SENIOR YEAR

Employer:

Job Description:

Dates:

Summer Experiences

FRESHMAN YEAR

Dates:

Description:

Dates:

Description:

Dates:

Description:

Dates:

Description:

Dates:

Description:

Summer Experiences

SOPHOMORE YEAR

Dates:

Description:

Dates:

Description:

Dates:

Description:

Dates:

Description:

Dates:

Description:

Summer Experiences

JUNIOR YEAR

Dates:

Description:

Dates:

Description:

Dates:

Description:

Dates:

Description:

Dates:

Description:

Summer Experiences

SENIOR YEAR

Dates:

Description:

Dates:

Description:

Dates:

Description:

Dates:

Description:

Dates:

Description:

Letters of Recommendation

Name:

Address:

Email:

Telephone: Date Requested:

Name:

Address:

Email:

Telephone: Date Requested:

Name:

Address:

Email:

Telephone: Date Requested:

Name:

Address:

Email:

Telephone: Date Requested:

CHAPTER 3

TESTING A TO Z: TRACK YOUR SCORES

By now you have become familiar with the alphabet soup of standardized tests: SAT, ACT, SAT Subject Tests, AP, IB, TOEFL. As you start to think about schools that interest you, check out which tests they require. Some schools want the SAT, some want the ACT, while some accept either. Some want two SAT Subject Tests (commonly known as the SAT II) and a few want three. And some want no tests at all!

As you determine the tests you need to take, it's important to maintain a master test schedule, identifying the test, test date, registration deadlines, and location you register for. Not all tests are offered on every test date. Make sure to cover your bases—plan ahead!

"With multiple deadlines and tasks to keep on top of, it's easy for something to fall through the cracks."

–LAURA A. BRUNO, Associate Director of Admissions, York College, The City University of New York

ACT and SAT registration requires you to submit a photograph of yourself for security purposes. Have a current photo on hand when you sign up for your tests. Once your registration is complete, print your admission ticket. Enter the test-related details on the **Standardized Test Schedule**, label one of your 13 folders "General," and then file the ticket in that folder. The last thing you need on test morning is a desperate scramble.

The night before the SAT, as John S. frantically searched for his registration ticket, he realized he had never hit the "submit" button. After a sleepless night, he and his mother rushed to the test center and, in a frenzy, completed the necessary forms to secure a spot on the stand-by list.

On that note, remember to bring a calculator, sharpened number 2 pencils, and the required form of ID. Otherwise, it will be a long ride home.

Once you have your results, record all test dates and corresponding scores on the **Standardized Test Scores** forms provided in this chapter. These forms provide an organized and easily accessible format to list your test scores. It's important to highlight the highest individual section scores you have earned—even if those scores are from different test dates. Should you opt to take a test that is not included in these forms, use the space provided on page 63 to record those results.

From this list, you will select your top scores to send to each school. This is your record of the scores you will submit in support of your application. File your Standardized Test Scores forms in your **General** folder, as you may need to refer to them again—it's not unusual for schools to misplace scores, and this will help you respond promptly to any additional requests.

There are several ways to submit your scores to the colleges you are applying to. You can opt to take advantage of the free score reports that the College Board and ACT offer when you register for the tests. In addition, at a later date, you can request to submit your scores by phone or online. Payment or a fee waiver is required before test scores are forwarded. Make sure to pay attention to application deadlines so your scores are submitted on time.

If you're considering applying to a test-optional school, please note that these schools may request a graded writing sample with teacher comments. Now is a good time to look through those old assignments cluttering your desk and locate a paper you're proud of. File the paper in the **General** folder.

Standardized Test Schedule

Test Date	Test	Location

Standardized Test Scores

SAT

DATE	CRITICAL READING	MATH	WRITING	OVERALL

SAT SUBJECT TESTS

SUBJECT:	
Date:	Score:
Date:	Score:

SUBJECT:	
Date:	Score:
Date:	Score:

SUBJECT:	
Date:	Score:
Date:	Score:

SUBJECT:	
Date:	Score:
Date:	Score:

ACT

DATE	ENGLISH	MATH	READING	SCIENCE	WRITING	COMPOSITE

OTHER TESTS

SUBJECT:	
Date:	Score:
Date:	Score:

SUBJECT:	
Date:	Score:
Date:	Score:

SUBJECT:	
Date:	Score:
Date:	Score:

ADVANCED PLACEMENT/INTERNATIONAL BACCALAUREATE EXAMS

DATE	SUBJECT	SCORE

TOEFL

DATE	LISTENING	READING	WRITING	SPEAKING

CHAPTER 4

RESEARCHING SCHOOLS: GETTING ACQUAINTED

Is there one perfect college or university for you? Perhaps. Most likely, though, there are many schools that could be a great fit. However, every school has its own unique personality. Whether visiting online, on campus, or meeting with a school representative or alumnus, you'll sense the distinct characteristics that differentiate one school from another.

Making a list of colleges to explore is a significant step—there are so many factors to consider. Talk to your parents and guidance counselor, and research schools on your own, so that you can compile a list that meets both your academic and personal requirements. Creating a balanced list of safety, target, and reach schools will offer you a number of alternatives to choose from at decision time.

> "If you conduct your proper research to find out the academic profiles and requirements of the colleges you are interested in, heed the advice of your school counselors, and take the time to visit the colleges that you are considering, you will most likely find that after the application and admissions process is complete, you will be happy with the results. If you are honest with yourself and honest with the process, you will most likely find out that you end up at the college where you belong!"
>
> —KEVIN O'SULLIVAN, Director of Undergraduate Admissions, Manhattanville College

In this section, you will record your reactions to the schools you investigate. Fifteen copies of each *Getting Acquainted* worksheet are provided—use one for each school you research.

- If you visit a school, take note of its distinguishing characteristics.
- How large is the school, both physically and in terms of the student body?
- How would you describe the surrounding neighborhood?
- Would you be happy living in this location for the next four years?
- List special academic programs and extracurricular activities that particularly interest you.
- If possible, arrange to sit in on a class.
- Note your reactions to the social atmosphere on campus.

- Is the cost to attend a school within your family's budget? Use the Net Price Calculator on each school's website to determine your estimated cost to attend.

- Remember, your personal response to the school and your impressions will help you determine your fit. Though it may sound tedious, write down memorable conversations and your gut reactions. It will be helpful to review these when you look back on all of your visits. It's important to jot down this information promptly because it's easy to confuse details about dorms, food courts, clubs, and special programs from one campus and website to another.

Prior to school visits, record the date, time, and location of tours and information sessions. Does the school offer the opportunity for on-campus interviews? If so, schedule your interview to fit in with the other on-campus events you plan to attend. Take the time to research: visit school websites, review course offerings, and prepare questions for representatives and tour guides. Find out if there's an opportunity to have lunch with students, download a class schedule, or even sign up to stay overnight. Also check if the school is in session. Most colleges still offer tours during school vacation, but there may be fewer students to see and talk to. Many schools offer and/or require interviews with alumni in your home town. Check the school's website to know whether the alumnus will contact you or if you are responsible for scheduling an interview.

> **"I would also tell students how important it is to demonstrate interest in the college they are applying to, especially if that school is a top choice.**
>
> **We will document if a student has interacted with our staff directly through email conversations, phone conversations, campus tours, information sessions, and personal interviews with a staff member."**
>
> —NICOLE KELMAN, Assistant Director of Admission, Muhlenberg College

The people you meet during this investigative stage may be contacts you wish to reach out to later in the application process. Enter names and contact information of individuals, including tour guides, admissions office representatives, professors, and coaches on the forms in this chapter.

My son's tour guide at one campus we visited became an email buddy and a great source of "insider" information about the particular program he was interested in.

> **"Aim to maintain consistent communication with the colleges and universities of your choice. Build a relationship with the admissions officer that travels to your region. Set up interviews if possible. Speak with the representative at a fair or when they visit your high school; take their business card, and follow up. Visit, take a tour, and sit in on an information session. Attend Open Houses if they are available. If you cannot visit (i.e., distance) ask for an alumni interview."**
>
> —ZEE SANTIAGO, Assistant Director of Admissions, Trinity College

Maintain a separate **Correspondence Journal** for each school you apply to. This log enables you to record the names and dates of your correspondence for easy and quick reference. In the early stages of the application process, your correspondence may be for fact-finding. However, as the process progresses, you may need to update your admissions file or contact a representative in support of your application. Deferral and waitlist decisions may require you to provide supplemental information as well. Print hard copies of written or electronic correspondence to file in the individual school folders you'll be creating shortly.

> **"Most schools will alert you when your file is complete. If they do so in writing or by email, keep a record of these contacts. If you have not heard from a school, contact them and note the date/time of contact and the name of the person with whom you spoke."**
>
> —ALISON ALMASIAN, Director of Admissions, St. Lawrence University

> **"We welcome questions by either email or telephone, depending on what works best for you. Since high school students tend to be in school during regular business hours, many students find email to be a more practical way of reaching their counselors."**
>
> —JIM ROGERS, Dean of Admission, Marymount Manhattan College

All *Getting Acquainted* forms should remain in the book until you're ready to compile your master list of schools. Once you create corresponding folders, you'll file all relevant forms in these individual school folders.

School Search

On-Campus Visit/Online Research

Name of School:

Address:

Date of Campus Visit:

TOUR GUIDE:

_____

Telephone:_____

Email:_____

INFORMATION SESSION LEADER:

_____

Telephone:_____

Email:_____

ADMISSIONS REGIONAL REPRESENTATIVE:

_____

Telephone:_____

Email:_____

BASIC FACTS

Community (circle):   urban   suburban   rural

Surrounding neighborhood:_____

Distance from home: _____miles   Accessibility (circle):   car   train   plane

Transportation costs: $_____   Average total cost per year: $_____

Your estimated cost to attend: $_____

(use the **NET PRICE CALCULATOR** on the school's website)

FACILITIES

Housing options (singles, doubles, suites, co-ed? guaranteed?):

Dining halls:

Student center:

Athletic facilities/fitness center:

Cultural event space (theaters, galleries…):

Student health services:

Buildings and grounds:

Look around! If time allows, have lunch at a dining hall Are students socializing, are they engaged in conversation, or are they studying?

STUDENT BODY

Size:_____

Male/female ratio:_____

Diversity:_____

Academic atmosphere:_____

School spirit:_____

Temperament (friendly, helpful…):_____

Undergraduate versus graduate population:_____

Try to strike up a conversation with a current student.

Average SAT score:_____

Average ACT score:_____

Average GPA:_____

ACADEMICS

Student/faculty ratio:

_____

Classes taught by professors versus teaching assistants:

_____

Average class size:

_____

Classrooms/labs/support facilities:

_____

Popular majors/programs:

_____

Library(-ies):

_____

Availability of tutoring:

_____

Advisory support:

_____

Career counseling/placement:

_____

Study abroad opportunities:

_____

If you attend a class, try to chat with the professor before or after.

EXTRACURRICULAR ACTIVITIES

Greek life:

_____

Clubs:

_____

Athletics (club, intramural):

_____

Availability of religious services:

_____

Community service opportunities:

_____

Cultural events:

_____

Other activities that interest you:

Notable points made by admissions representatives:

What did you learn from your tour guide?

Outstanding memories:

Reasons you're interested in this school:

School Search

On-Campus Visit/Online Research

Name of School: _____

Address: _____

Date of Campus Visit: _____

TOUR GUIDE:

_____

Telephone:_____

Email:_____

INFORMATION SESSION LEADER:

_____

Telephone:_____

Email:_____

ADMISSIONS REGIONAL REPRESENTATIVE:

_____

Telephone:_____

Email:_____

BASIC FACTS

Community (circle):   urban   suburban   rural

Surrounding neighborhood:_____

Distance from home: _____miles   Accessibility (circle):   car   train   plane

Transportation costs: $_____   Average total cost per year: $_____

Your estimated cost to attend: $_____

(use the **NET PRICE CALCULATOR** on the school's website)

FACILITIES

Housing options (singles, doubles, suites, co-ed? guaranteed?):

Dining halls:

Student center:

Athletic facilities/fitness center:

Cultural event space (theaters, galleries...):

Student health services:

Buildings and grounds:

Look around! If time allows, have lunch at a dining hall. Are students socializing, are they engaged in conversation, or are they studying?

STUDENT BODY

Size:_____

Male/female ratio:_____

Diversity:_____

Academic atmosphere:_____

School spirit:_____

Temperament (friendly, helpful...):_____

Undergraduate versus graduate population:_____

Try to strike up a conversation with a current student.

Average SAT score:_____

Average ACT score:_____

Average GPA:_____

ACADEMICS

Student/faculty ratio:

_____

Classes taught by professors versus teaching assistants:

_____

Average class size:

_____

Classrooms/labs/support facilities:

_____

Popular majors/programs:

_____

Library(-ies):

_____

Availability of tutoring:

_____

Advisory support:

_____

Career counseling/placement:

_____

Study abroad opportunities:

_____

If you attend a class, try to chat with the professor before or after.

EXTRACURRICULAR ACTIVITIES

Greek life:

_____

Clubs:

_____

Athletics (club, intramural):

_____

Availability of religious services:

_____

Community service opportunities:

_____

Cultural events:

_____

Other activities that interest you:

Notable points made by admissions representatives:

What did you learn from your tour guide?

Outstanding memories:

Reasons you're interested in this school:

School Search

On-Campus Visit/Online Research

TOUR GUIDE:

_____

Telephone:_____

Email:_____

INFORMATION SESSION LEADER:

_____

Telephone:_____

Email:_____

ADMISSIONS REGIONAL REPRESENTATIVE:

_____

Telephone:_____

Email:_____

Name of School:

Address:

Date of Campus Visit:

BASIC FACTS

Community (circle):   urban   suburban   rural

Surrounding neighborhood:_____

Distance from home: _____miles   Accessibility (circle):   car   train   plane

Transportation costs: $_____   Average total cost per year: $_____

Your estimated cost to attend: $_____

(use the **NET PRICE CALCULATOR** on the school's website)

FACILITIES

Housing options (singles, doubles, suites, co-ed? guaranteed?):

Dining halls:

Student center:

Athletic facilities/fitness center:

Cultural event space (theaters, galleries...):

Student health services:

Buildings and grounds:

Look around! If time allows, have lunch at a dining hall. Are students socializing, are they engaged in conversation, or are they studying?

STUDENT BODY

Size:_____

Male/female ratio:_____

Diversity:_____

Academic atmosphere:_____

School spirit:_____

Temperament (friendly, helpful...):_____

Undergraduate versus graduate population:_____

Try to strike up a conversation with a current student.

Average SAT score:_____

Average ACT score:_____

Average GPA:_____

ACADEMICS

Student/faculty ratio:

_____

Classes taught by professors versus teaching assistants:

_____

Average class size:

_____

Classrooms/labs/support facilities:

_____

Popular majors/programs:

_____

Library(-ies):

_____

Availability of tutoring:

_____

Advisory support:

_____

Career counseling/placement:

_____

Study abroad opportunities:

_____

If you attend a class, try to chat with the professor before or after.

EXTRACURRICULAR ACTIVITIES

Greek life:

_____

Clubs:

_____

Athletics (club, intramural):

_____

Availability of religious services:

_____

Community service opportunities:

_____

Cultural events:

_____

Other activities that interest you:

Notable points made by admissions representatives:

What did you learn from your tour guide?

Outstanding memories:

Reasons you're interested in this school:

School Search

On-Campus Visit/Online Research

Name of School:

Address:

Date of Campus Visit:

TOUR GUIDE:

_____

    Telephone:_____

    Email:_____

INFORMATION SESSION LEADER:

_____

    Telephone:_____

    Email:_____

ADMISSIONS REGIONAL REPRESENTATIVE:

_____

    Telephone:_____

    Email:_____

BASIC FACTS

    Community (circle): urban   suburban   rural

    Surrounding neighborhood:_____

    Distance from home: _____miles Accessibility (circle): car   train   plane

    Transportation costs: $_____ Average total cost per year: $_____

    Your estimated cost to attend: $_____

    (use the **NET PRICE CALCULATOR** on the school's website)

FACILITIES

Housing options (singles, doubles, suites, co-ed? guaranteed?):

Dining halls:

Student center:

Athletic facilities/fitness center:

Cultural event space (theaters, galleries…):

Student health services:

Buildings and grounds:

Look around! If time allows, have lunch at a dining hall Are students socializing, are they engaged in conversation, or are they studying?

STUDENT BODY

Size:_____

Male/female ratio:_____

Diversity:_____

Academic atmosphere:_____

School spirit:_____

Temperament (friendly, helpful…):_____

Undergraduate versus graduate population:_____

Try to strike up a conversation with a current student.

Average SAT score:_____

Average ACT score:_____

Average GPA:_____

ACADEMICS

Student/faculty ratio:

_____

Classes taught by professors versus teaching assistants:

_____

Average class size:

_____

Classrooms/labs/support facilities:

_____

Popular majors/programs:

_____

Library(-ies):

_____

Availability of tutoring:

_____

Advisory support:

_____

Career counseling/placement:

_____

Study abroad opportunities:

_____

If you attend a class, try to chat with the professor before or after.

EXTRACURRICULAR ACTIVITIES

Greek life:

_____

Clubs:

_____

Athletics (club, intramural):

_____

Availability of religious services:

_____

Community service opportunities:

_____

Cultural events:

_____

Other activities that interest you:

_____

_____

_____

_____

_____

_____

_____

_____

_____

_____

Notable points made by admissions representatives:

What did you learn from your tour guide?

Outstanding memories:

Reasons you're interested in this school:

School Search

On-Campus Visit/Online Research

TOUR GUIDE:

_____

Telephone:_____

Email:_____

INFORMATION SESSION LEADER:

_____

Telephone:_____

Email:_____

ADMISSIONS REGIONAL REPRESENTATIVE:

_____

Telephone:_____

Email:_____

Name of School:

Address:

Date of Campus Visit:

BASIC FACTS

Community (circle):   urban   suburban   rural

Surrounding neighborhood:_____

Distance from home: _____miles   Accessibility (circle):   car   train   plane

Transportation costs: $_____   Average total cost per year: $_____

Your estimated cost to attend: $_____

(use the **NET PRICE CALCULATOR** on the school's website)

FACILITIES

Housing options (singles, doubles, suites, co-ed? guaranteed?):

Dining halls:

Student center:

Athletic facilities/fitness center:

Cultural event space (theaters, galleries…):

Student health services:

Buildings and grounds:

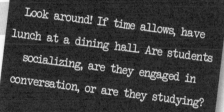

Look around! If time allows, have lunch at a dining hall. Are students socializing, are they engaged in conversation, or are they studying?

STUDENT BODY

Size:_____

Male/female ratio:_____

Diversity:_____

Academic atmosphere:_____

School spirit:_____

Temperament (friendly, helpful…):_____

Undergraduate versus graduate population:_____

Average SAT score:_____

Average ACT score:_____

Average GPA:_____

Try to strike up a conversation with a current student.

ACADEMICS

Student/faculty ratio:

_____

Classes taught by professors versus teaching assistants:

_____

Average class size:

_____

Classrooms/labs/support facilities:

_____

Popular majors/programs:

_____

Library(-ies):

_____

Availability of tutoring:

_____

Advisory support:

_____

Career counseling/placement:

_____

Study abroad opportunities:

_____

If you attend a class, try to chat with the professor before or after.

EXTRACURRICULAR ACTIVITIES

Greek life:

_____

Clubs:

_____

Athletics (club, intramural):

_____

Availability of religious services:

_____

Community service opportunities:

_____

Cultural events:

_____

Other activities that interest you:

Notable points made by admissions representatives:

What did you learn from your tour guide?

Outstanding memories:

Reasons you're interested in this school:

School Search

On-Campus Visit/Online Research

Name of School: _____

Address: _____

Date of Campus Visit: _____

TOUR GUIDE:

_____

Telephone:_____

Email:_____

INFORMATION SESSION LEADER:

_____

Telephone:_____

Email:_____

ADMISSIONS REGIONAL REPRESENTATIVE:

_____

Telephone:_____

Email:_____

BASIC FACTS

Community (circle):   urban   suburban   rural

Surrounding neighborhood:_____

Distance from home: _____miles   Accessibility (circle):   car   train   plane

Transportation costs: $_____   Average total cost per year: $_____

Your estimated cost to attend: $_____

(use the **NET PRICE CALCULATOR** on the school's website)

FACILITIES

Housing options (singles, doubles, suites, co-ed? guaranteed?):

Dining halls:

Student center:

Athletic facilities/fitness center:

Cultural event space (theaters, galleries…):

Student health services:

Buildings and grounds:

Look around! If time allows, have lunch at a dining hall. Are students socializing, are they engaged in conversation, or are they studying?

STUDENT BODY

Size:_____

Male/female ratio:_____

Diversity:_____

Academic atmosphere:_____

School spirit:_____

Temperament (friendly, helpful…):_____

Undergraduate versus graduate population:_____

Average SAT score:_____

Average ACT score:_____

Try to strike up a conversation with a current student.

Average GPA:_____

ACADEMICS

Student/faculty ratio:

_____

Classes taught by professors versus teaching assistants:

_____

Average class size:

_____

Classrooms/labs/support facilities:

_____

Popular majors/programs:

_____

Library(-ies):

_____

Availability of tutoring:

_____

Advisory support:

_____

Career counseling/placement:

_____

Study abroad opportunities:

_____

If you attend a class, try to chat with the professor before or after.

EXTRACURRICULAR ACTIVITIES

Greek life:

_____

Clubs:

_____

Athletics (club, intramural):

_____

Availability of religious services:

_____

Community service opportunities:

_____

Cultural events:

_____

Other activities that interest you:

Notable points made by admissions representatives:

What did you learn from your tour guide?

Outstanding memories:

Reasons you're interested in this school:

School Search

On-Campus Visit/Online Research

Name of School:

Address:

Date of Campus Visit:

TOUR GUIDE:

_____

Telephone:_____

Email:_____

INFORMATION SESSION LEADER:

_____

Telephone:_____

Email:_____

ADMISSIONS REGIONAL REPRESENTATIVE:

_____

Telephone:_____

Email:_____

BASIC FACTS

Community (circle):   urban   suburban   rural

Surrounding neighborhood:_____

Distance from home: _____miles   Accessibility (circle):   car   train   plane

Transportation costs: $_____ Average total cost per year: $_____

Your estimated cost to attend: $_____

(use the **NET PRICE CALCULATOR** on the school's website)

FACILITIES

Housing options (singles, doubles, suites, co-ed? guaranteed?):

Dining halls:

Student center:

Athletic facilities/fitness center:

Cultural event space (theaters, galleries…):

Student health services:

Buildings and grounds:

Look around! If time allows, have lunch at a dining hall Are students socializing, are they engaged in conversation, or are they studying?

STUDENT BODY

Size:_____

Male/female ratio:_____

Diversity:_____

Academic atmosphere:_____

School spirit:_____

Temperament (friendly, helpful…):_____

Undergraduate versus graduate population:_____

Try to strike up a conversation with a current student.

Average SAT score:_____

Average ACT score:_____

Average GPA:_____

ACADEMICS

Student/faculty ratio:

_____

Classes taught by professors versus teaching assistants:

_____

Average class size:

_____

Classrooms/labs/support facilities:

_____

Popular majors/programs:

_____

Library(-ies):

_____

Availability of tutoring:

_____

Advisory support:

_____

Career counseling/placement:

_____

Study abroad opportunities:

_____

If you attend a class, try to chat with the professor before or after.

EXTRACURRICULAR ACTIVITIES

Greek life:

_____

Clubs:

_____

Athletics (club, intramural):

_____

Availability of religious services:

_____

Community service opportunities:

_____

Cultural events:

_____

Other activities that interest you:

Notable points made by admissions representatives:

What did you learn from your tour guide?

Outstanding memories:

Reasons you're interested in this school:

School Search

On-Campus Visit/Online Research

Name of School:

Address:

Date of Campus Visit:

TOUR GUIDE:

_____

Telephone:_____

Email:_____

INFORMATION SESSION LEADER:

_____

Telephone:_____

Email:_____

ADMISSIONS REGIONAL REPRESENTATIVE:

_____

Telephone:_____

Email:_____

BASIC FACTS

Community (circle):   urban   suburban   rural

Surrounding neighborhood:_____

Distance from home: _____miles   Accessibility (circle):   car   train   plane

Transportation costs: $_____   Average total cost per year: $_____

Your estimated cost to attend: $_____

(use the **NET PRICE CALCULATOR** on the school's website)

FACILITIES

Housing options (singles, doubles, suites, co-ed? guaranteed?):

Dining halls:

Student center:

Athletic facilities/fitness center:

Cultural event space (theaters, galleries…):

Student health services:

Buildings and grounds:

Look around! If time allows, have lunch at a dining hall. Are students socializing, are they engaged in conversation, or are they studying?

STUDENT BODY

Size:_____

Male/female ratio:_____

Diversity:_____

Academic atmosphere:_____

School spirit:_____

Temperament (friendly, helpful…):_____

Undergraduate versus graduate population:_____

Average SAT score:_____

Average ACT score:_____

Average GPA:_____

Try to strike up a conversation with a current student.

ACADEMICS

Student/faculty ratio:

_____

Classes taught by professors versus teaching assistants:

_____

Average class size:

_____

Classrooms/labs/support facilities:

_____

Popular majors/programs:

_____

Library(-ies):

_____

Availability of tutoring:

_____

Advisory support:

_____

Career counseling/placement:

_____

Study abroad opportunities:

_____

If you attend a class, try to chat with the professor before or after.

EXTRACURRICULAR ACTIVITIES

Greek life:

_____

Clubs:

_____

Athletics (club, intramural):

_____

Availability of religious services:

_____

Community service opportunities:

_____

Cultural events:

_____

Other activities that interest you:

Notable points made by admissions representatives:

What did you learn from your tour guide?

Outstanding memories:

Reasons you're interested in this school:

School Search

On-Campus Visit/Online Research

Name of School:

Address:

Date of Campus Visit:

TOUR GUIDE:

_____

Telephone:_____

Email:_____

INFORMATION SESSION LEADER:

_____

Telephone:_____

Email:_____

ADMISSIONS REGIONAL REPRESENTATIVE:

_____

Telephone:_____

Email:_____

BASIC FACTS

Community (circle):   urban   suburban   rural

Surrounding neighborhood:_____

Distance from home: _____miles   Accessibility (circle):   car   train   plane

Transportation costs: $_____   Average total cost per year: $_____

Your estimated cost to attend: $_____

(use the **NET PRICE CALCULATOR** on the school's website)

FACILITIES

Housing options (singles, doubles, suites, co-ed? guaranteed?):

Dining halls:

Student center:

Athletic facilities/fitness center:

Cultural event space (theaters, galleries...):

Student health services:

Buildings and grounds:

> Look around! If time allows, have lunch at a dining hall Are students socializing, are they engaged in conversation, or are they studying?

STUDENT BODY

Size:_____

Male/female ratio:_____

Diversity:_____

Academic atmosphere:_____

School spirit:_____

Temperament (friendly, helpful...):_____

Undergraduate versus graduate population:_____

> Try to strike up a conversation with a current student.

Average SAT score:_____

Average ACT score:_____

Average GPA:_____

ACADEMICS

Student/faculty ratio:

_____

Classes taught by professors versus teaching assistants:

_____

Average class size:

_____

Classrooms/labs/support facilities:

_____

Popular majors/programs:

_____

Library(-ies):

_____

Availability of tutoring:

_____

Advisory support:

_____

Career counseling/placement:

_____

Study abroad opportunities:

_____

If you attend a class, try to chat with the professor before or after.

EXTRACURRICULAR ACTIVITIES

Greek life:

_____

Clubs:

_____

Athletics (club, intramural):

_____

Availability of religious services:

_____

Community service opportunities:

_____

Cultural events:

_____

Other activities that interest you:

Notable points made by admissions representatives:

What did you learn from your tour guide?

Outstanding memories:

Reasons you're interested in this school:

School Search

On-Campus Visit/Online Research

TOUR GUIDE:

_____

Telephone:_____

Email:_____

INFORMATION SESSION LEADER:

_____

Telephone:_____

Email:_____

ADMISSIONS REGIONAL REPRESENTATIVE:

_____

Telephone:_____

Email:_____

Name of School:

Address:

Date of Campus Visit:

BASIC FACTS

Community (circle):   urban   suburban   rural

Surrounding neighborhood:_____

Distance from home: _____miles   Accessibility (circle):   car   train   plane

Transportation costs: $_____ Average total cost per year: $_____

Your estimated cost to attend: $_____

(use the **NET PRICE CALCULATOR** on the school's website)

FACILITIES

Housing options (singles, doubles, suites, co-ed? guaranteed?):

Dining halls:

Student center:

Athletic facilities/fitness center:

Cultural event space (theaters, galleries…):

Student health services:

Buildings and grounds:

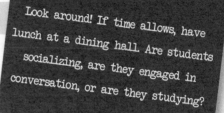

Look around! If time allows, have lunch at a dining hall. Are students socializing, are they engaged in conversation, or are they studying?

STUDENT BODY

Size:_____

Male/female ratio:_____

Diversity:_____

Academic atmosphere:_____

School spirit:_____

Temperament (friendly, helpful…):_____

Undergraduate versus graduate population:_____

Try to strike up a conversation with a current student.

Average SAT score:_____

Average ACT score:_____

Average GPA:_____

ACADEMICS

Student/faculty ratio:

_____

Classes taught by professors versus teaching assistants:

_____

Average class size:

_____

Classrooms/labs/support facilities:

_____

Popular majors/programs:

_____

Library(-ies):

_____

Availability of tutoring:

_____

Advisory support:

_____

Career counseling/placement:

_____

Study abroad opportunities:

_____

If you attend a class, try to chat with the professor before or after.

EXTRACURRICULAR ACTIVITIES

Greek life:

_____

Clubs:

_____

Athletics (club, intramural):

_____

Availability of religious services:

_____

Community service opportunities:

_____

Cultural events:

_____

Other activities that interest you:

Notable points made by admissions representatives:

What did you learn from your tour guide?

Outstanding memories:

Reasons you're interested in this school:

School Search

On-Campus Visit/Online Research

Name of School:

Address:

Date of Campus Visit:

TOUR GUIDE:

_____

Telephone:_____

Email:_____

INFORMATION SESSION LEADER:

_____

Telephone:_____

Email:_____

ADMISSIONS REGIONAL REPRESENTATIVE:

_____

Telephone:_____

Email:_____

BASIC FACTS

Community (circle):   urban   suburban   rural

Surrounding neighborhood:_____

Distance from home: _____miles   Accessibility (circle):   car   train   plane

Transportation costs: $_____   Average total cost per year: $_____

Your estimated cost to attend: $_____

(use the **NET PRICE CALCULATOR** on the school's website)

FACILITIES

Housing options (singles, doubles, suites, co-ed? guaranteed?):

Dining halls:

Student center:

Athletic facilities/fitness center:

Cultural event space (theaters, galleries…):

Student health services:

Buildings and grounds:

Look around! If time allows, have lunch at a dining hall. Are students socializing, are they engaged in conversation, or are they studying?

STUDENT BODY

Size:_____

Male/female ratio:_____

Diversity:_____

Academic atmosphere:_____

School spirit:_____

Temperament (friendly, helpful…):_____

Undergraduate versus graduate population:_____

Try to strike up a conversation with a current student.

Average SAT score:_____

Average ACT score:_____

Average GPA:_____

ACADEMICS

Student/faculty ratio:

_____

Classes taught by professors versus teaching assistants:

_____

Average class size:

_____

Classrooms/labs/support facilities:

_____

Popular majors/programs:

_____

Library(-ies):

_____

Availability of tutoring:

_____

Advisory support:

_____

Career counseling/placement:

_____

Study abroad opportunities:

_____

If you attend a class, try to chat with the professor before or after.

EXTRACURRICULAR ACTIVITIES

Greek life:

_____

Clubs:

_____

Athletics (club, intramural):

_____

Availability of religious services:

_____

Community service opportunities:

_____

Cultural events:

_____

Other activities that interest you:

Notable points made by admissions representatives:

What did you learn from your tour guide?

Outstanding memories:

Reasons you're interested in this school:

School Search

On-Campus Visit/Online Research

Name of School:

Address:

Date of Campus Visit:

TOUR GUIDE:

_____

Telephone:_____

Email:_____

INFORMATION SESSION LEADER:

_____

Telephone:_____

Email:_____

ADMISSIONS REGIONAL REPRESENTATIVE:

_____

Telephone:_____

Email:_____

BASIC FACTS

Community (circle):   urban   suburban   rural

Surrounding neighborhood:_____

Distance from home: _____miles   Accessibility (circle):   car   train   plane

Transportation costs: $_____   Average total cost per year: $_____

Your estimated cost to attend: $_____

(use the **NET PRICE CALCULATOR** on the school's website)

FACILITIES

Housing options (singles, doubles, suites, co-ed? guaranteed?):

Dining halls:

Student center:

Athletic facilities/fitness center:

Cultural event space (theaters, galleries…):

Student health services:

Buildings and grounds:

Look around! If time allows, have lunch at a dining hall. Are students socializing, are they engaged in conversation, or are they studying?

STUDENT BODY

Size:_____

Male/female ratio:_____

Diversity:_____

Academic atmosphere:_____

School spirit:_____

Temperament (friendly, helpful…):_____

Undergraduate versus graduate population:_____

Try to strike up a conversation with a current student.

Average SAT score:_____

Average ACT score:_____

Average GPA:_____

ACADEMICS

Student/faculty ratio:

_____

Classes taught by professors versus teaching assistants:

_____

Average class size:

_____

Classrooms/labs/support facilities:

_____

Popular majors/programs:

_____

Library(-ies):

_____

Availability of tutoring:

_____

Advisory support:

_____

Career counseling/placement:

_____

Study abroad opportunities:

_____

If you attend a class, try to chat with the professor before or after.

EXTRACURRICULAR ACTIVITIES

Greek life:

_____

Clubs:

_____

Athletics (club, intramural):

_____

Availability of religious services:

_____

Community service opportunities:

_____

Cultural events:

_____

Other activities that interest you:

Notable points made by admissions representatives:

What did you learn from your tour guide?

Outstanding memories:

Reasons you're interested in this school:

School Search

On-Campus Visit/Online Research

TOUR GUIDE:

_____

    Telephone:_____

    Email:_____

INFORMATION SESSION LEADER:

_____

    Telephone:_____

    Email:_____

ADMISSIONS REGIONAL REPRESENTATIVE:

_____

    Telephone:_____

    Email:_____

BASIC FACTS

    Community (circle): urban   suburban   rural

    Surrounding neighborhood:_____

    Distance from home: _____miles Accessibility (circle): car   train   plane

    Transportation costs: $_____ Average total cost per year: $_____

    Your estimated cost to attend: $_____

    (use the **NET PRICE CALCULATOR** on the school's website)

FACILITIES

Housing options (singles, doubles, suites, co-ed? guaranteed?):

Dining halls:

Student center:

Athletic facilities/fitness center:

Cultural event space (theaters, galleries…):

Student health services:

Buildings and grounds:

Look around! If time allows, have lunch at a dining hall Are students socializing, are they engaged in conversation, or are they studying?

STUDENT BODY

Size:

Male/female ratio:

Diversity:

Academic atmosphere:

School spirit:

Temperament (friendly, helpful…):

Undergraduate versus graduate population:

Average SAT score:

Average ACT score:

Average GPA:

Try to strike up a conversation with a current student.

ACADEMICS

Student/faculty ratio:

_____

Classes taught by professors versus teaching assistants:

_____

Average class size:

_____

Classrooms/labs/support facilities:

_____

Popular majors/programs:

_____

Library(-ies):

_____

Availability of tutoring:

_____

Advisory support:

_____

Career counseling/placement:

_____

Study abroad opportunities:

_____

If you attend a class, try to chat with the professor before or after.

EXTRACURRICULAR ACTIVITIES

Greek life:

_____

Clubs:

_____

Athletics (club, intramural):

_____

Availability of religious services:

_____

Community service opportunities:

_____

Cultural events:

_____

Other activities that interest you:

Notable points made by admissions representatives:

What did you learn from your tour guide?

Outstanding memories:

Reasons you're interested in this school:

School Search

On-Campus Visit/Online Research

TOUR GUIDE:

_____

Telephone:_____

Email:_____

INFORMATION SESSION LEADER:

_____

Telephone:_____

Email:_____

ADMISSIONS REGIONAL REPRESENTATIVE:

_____

Telephone:_____

Email:_____

Name of School:

Address:

Date of Campus Visit:

BASIC FACTS

Community (circle):   urban   suburban   rural

Surrounding neighborhood:_____

Distance from home: _____miles   Accessibility (circle):   car   train   plane

Transportation costs: $_____   Average total cost per year: $_____

Your estimated cost to attend: $_____

(use the **NET PRICE CALCULATOR** on the school's website)

FACILITIES

Housing options (singles, doubles, suites, co-ed? guaranteed?):

Dining halls:

Student center:

Athletic facilities/fitness center:

Cultural event space (theaters, galleries…):

Student health services:

Buildings and grounds:

> Look around! If time allows, have lunch at a dining hall. Are students socializing, are they engaged in conversation, or are they studying?

STUDENT BODY

Size:_____

Male/female ratio:_____

Diversity:_____

Academic atmosphere:_____

School spirit:_____

Temperament (friendly, helpful…):_____

Undergraduate versus graduate population:_____

> Try to strike up a conversation with a current student.

Average SAT score:_____

Average ACT score:_____

Average GPA:_____

ACADEMICS

Student/faculty ratio:

_____

Classes taught by professors versus teaching assistants:

_____

Average class size:

_____

Classrooms/labs/support facilities:

_____

Popular majors/programs:

_____

Library(-ies):

_____

Availability of tutoring:

_____

Advisory support:

_____

Career counseling/placement:

_____

Study abroad opportunities:

_____

If you attend a class, try to chat with the professor before or after.

EXTRACURRICULAR ACTIVITIES

Greek life:

_____

Clubs:

_____

Athletics (club, intramural):

_____

Availability of religious services:

_____

Community service opportunities:

_____

Cultural events:

_____

Other activities that interest you:

Notable points made by admissions representatives:

What did you learn from your tour guide?

Outstanding memories:

Reasons you're interested in this school:

School Search

On-Campus Visit/Online Research

Name of School: _____

Address: _____

Date of Campus Visit: _____

TOUR GUIDE:

_____

Telephone:_____

Email:_____

INFORMATION SESSION LEADER:

_____

Telephone:_____

Email:_____

ADMISSIONS REGIONAL REPRESENTATIVE:

_____

Telephone:_____

Email:_____

BASIC FACTS

Community (circle): urban   suburban   rural

Surrounding neighborhood:_____

Distance from home: _____miles   Accessibility (circle): car   train   plane

Transportation costs: $_____   Average total cost per year: $_____

Your estimated cost to attend: $_____

(use the **NET PRICE CALCULATOR** on the school's website)

FACILITIES

Housing options (singles, doubles, suites, co-ed? guaranteed?):

Dining halls:

Student center:

Athletic facilities/fitness center:

Cultural event space (theaters, galleries…):

Student health services:

Buildings and grounds:

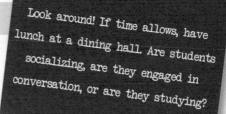

Look around! If time allows, have lunch at a dining hall. Are students socializing, are they engaged in conversation, or are they studying?

STUDENT BODY

Size:_____

Male/female ratio:_____

Diversity:_____

Academic atmosphere:_____

School spirit:_____

Temperament (friendly, helpful…):_____

Undergraduate versus graduate population:_____

Average SAT score:_____

Average ACT score:_____

Try to strike up a conversation with a current student.

Average GPA:_____

ACADEMICS

Student/faculty ratio:

_____

Classes taught by professors versus teaching assistants:

_____

Average class size:

_____

Classrooms/labs/support facilities:

_____

Popular majors/programs:

_____

Library(-ies):

_____

Availability of tutoring:

_____

Advisory support:

_____

Career counseling/placement:

_____

Study abroad opportunities:

_____

If you attend a class, try to chat with the professor before or after.

EXTRACURRICULAR ACTIVITIES

Greek life:

_____

Clubs:

_____

Athletics (club, intramural):

_____

Availability of religious services:

_____

Community service opportunities:

_____

Cultural events:

_____

Other activities that interest you:

Notable points made by admissions representatives:

What did you learn from your tour guide?

Outstanding memories:

Reasons you're interested in this school:

ON-CAMPUS INTERVIEWS

ADMISSIONS MEETING

Name:

Telephone Number: Date/time:

Email:

Location:

Notable information/impressions:

> Remember: Send a thank-you note to each person you meet.
>
> Enter all correspondence in your journal!

ADDITIONAL MEETING

Name:

Telephone Number: Date/time:

Email:

Location:

Notable information/impressions:

ADDITIONAL MEETING

Name:

Telephone Number: Date/time:

Email:

Location:

Notable information/impressions:

ON-CAMPUS INTERVIEWS

Name of School:

ADMISSIONS MEETING

Name:

Telephone Number: Date/time:

Email:

Location:

Notable information/impressions:

Remember: Send a thank-you note to each person you meet.

Enter all correspondence in your journal!

ADDITIONAL MEETING

Name:

Telephone Number: Date/time:

Email:

Location:

Notable information/impressions:

ADDITIONAL MEETING

Name:

Telephone Number: Date/time:

Email:

Location:

Notable information/impressions:

ON-CAMPUS INTERVIEWS

Name of School:

ADMISSIONS MEETING

Name:

Telephone Number: Date/time:

Email:

Location:

Notable information/impressions:

Remember: Send a thank-you note to each person you meet.

Enter all correspondence in your journal!

ADDITIONAL MEETING

Name:

Telephone Number: Date/time:

Email:

Location:

Notable information/impressions:

ADDITIONAL MEETING

Name:

Telephone Number: Date/time:

Email:

Location:

Notable information/impressions:

ON-CAMPUS INTERVIEWS

Name of School:

ADMISSIONS MEETING

Name:

Telephone Number: Date/time:

Email:

Location:

Notable information/impressions:

Remember: Send a thank-you note to each person you meet.

Enter all correspondence in your journal!

ADDITIONAL MEETING

Name:

Telephone Number: Date/time:

Email:

Location:

Notable information/impressions:

ADDITIONAL MEETING

Name:

Telephone Number: Date/time:

Email:

Location:

Notable information/impressions:

ON-CAMPUS INTERVIEWS

Name of School:

ADMISSIONS MEETING

Name:

Telephone Number: Date/time:

Email:

Location:

Notable information/impressions:

Remember: Send a thank-you note to each person you meet.

Enter all correspondence in your journal!

ADDITIONAL MEETING

Name:

Telephone Number: Date/time:

Email:

Location:

Notable information/impressions:

ADDITIONAL MEETING

Name:

Telephone Number: Date/time:

Email:

Location:

Notable information/impressions:

ON-CAMPUS INTERVIEWS

Name of School:

ADMISSIONS MEETING

Name:

Telephone Number: Date/time:

Email:

Location:

Notable information/impressions:

Remember: Send a thank-you note to each person you meet.

Enter all correspondence in your journal!

ADDITIONAL MEETING

Name:

Telephone Number: Date/time:

Email:

Location:

Notable information/impressions:

ADDITIONAL MEETING

Name:

Telephone Number: Date/time:

Email:

Location:

Notable information/impressions:

ON-CAMPUS INTERVIEWS

Name of School:

ADMISSIONS MEETING

Name:

Telephone Number: Date/time:

Email:

Location:

Notable information/impressions:

Remember: Send a thank-you note to each person you meet.

Enter all correspondence in your journal!

ADDITIONAL MEETING

Name:

Telephone Number: Date/time:

Email:

Location:

Notable information/impressions:

ADDITIONAL MEETING

Name:

Telephone Number: Date/time:

Email:

Location:

Notable information/impressions:

ON-CAMPUS INTERVIEWS

Name of School:

ADMISSIONS MEETING

Name:

Telephone Number: Date/time:

Email:

Location:

Notable information/impressions:

Remember: Send a thank-you note to each person you meet.

Enter all correspondence in your journal!

ADDITIONAL MEETING

Name:

Telephone Number: Date/time:

Email:

Location:

Notable information/impressions:

ADDITIONAL MEETING

Name:

Telephone Number: Date/time:

Email:

Location:

Notable information/impressions:

ON-CAMPUS INTERVIEWS

Name of School:

ADMISSIONS MEETING

Name:

Telephone Number: Date/time:

Email:

Location:

Notable information/impressions:

Remember: Send a thank-you note to each person you meet.

Enter all correspondence in your journal!

ADDITIONAL MEETING

Name:

Telephone Number: Date/time:

Email:

Location:

Notable information/impressions:

ADDITIONAL MEETING

Name:

Telephone Number: Date/time:

Email:

Location:

Notable information/impressions:

ON-CAMPUS INTERVIEWS

Name of School:

ADMISSIONS MEETING

Name:

Telephone Number: Date/time:

Email:

Location:

Notable information/impressions:

Remember: Send a thank-you note to each person you meet.

Enter all correspondence in your journal!

ADDITIONAL MEETING

Name:

Telephone Number: Date/time:

Email:

Location:

Notable information/impressions:

ADDITIONAL MEETING

Name:

Telephone Number: Date/time:

Email:

Location:

Notable information/impressions:

ON-CAMPUS INTERVIEWS

Name of School:

ADMISSIONS MEETING

Name:

Telephone Number: Date/time:

Email:

Location:

Notable information/impressions:

Remember: Send a thank-you note to each person you meet.

Enter all correspondence in your journal!

ADDITIONAL MEETING

Name:

Telephone Number: Date/time:

Email:

Location:

Notable information/impressions:

ADDITIONAL MEETING

Name:

Telephone Number: Date/time:

Email:

Location:

Notable information/impressions:

ON-CAMPUS INTERVIEWS

Name of School:

ADMISSIONS MEETING

Name:

Telephone Number: Date/time:

Email:

Location:

Notable information/impressions:

> Remember: Send a thank-you note to each person you meet.
>
> Enter all correspondence in your journal!

ADDITIONAL MEETING

Name:

Telephone Number: Date/time:

Email:

Location:

Notable information/impressions:

ADDITIONAL MEETING

Name:

Telephone Number: Date/time:

Email:

Location:

Notable information/impressions:

ON-CAMPUS INTERVIEWS

Name of School:

ADMISSIONS MEETING

Name:

Telephone Number: Date/time:

Email:

Location:

Notable information/impressions:

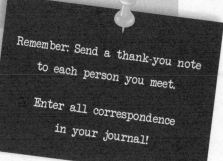

Remember: Send a thank-you note to each person you meet.

Enter all correspondence in your journal!

ADDITIONAL MEETING

Name:

Telephone Number: Date/time:

Email:

Location:

Notable information/impressions:

ADDITIONAL MEETING

Name:

Telephone Number: Date/time:

Email:

Location:

Notable information/impressions:

ON-CAMPUS INTERVIEWS

Name of School:

ADMISSIONS MEETING

Name:

Telephone Number: Date/time:

Email:

Location:

Notable information/impressions:

Remember: Send a thank-you note to each person you meet.

Enter all correspondence in your journal!

ADDITIONAL MEETING

Name:

Telephone Number: Date/time:

Email:

Location:

Notable information/impressions:

ADDITIONAL MEETING

Name:

Telephone Number: Date/time:

Email:

Location:

Notable information/impressions:

ON-CAMPUS INTERVIEWS

Name of School:

ADMISSIONS MEETING

Name:

Telephone Number: Date/time:

Email:

Location:

Notable information/impressions:

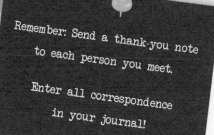

Remember: Send a thank-you note to each person you meet.

Enter all correspondence in your journal!

ADDITIONAL MEETING

Name:

Telephone Number: Date/time:

Email:

Location:

Notable information/impressions:

ADDITIONAL MEETING

Name:

Telephone Number: Date/time:

Email:

Location:

Notable information/impressions:

OFF-CAMPUS COLLEGE REP MEETING

Name of School:

COLLEGE REPRESENTATIVE

Name:

Telephone Number:

Email:

Date/time:

Location:

Notable information:

Is there any additional information you would like to request?

Remember that thank-you note!

OFF-CAMPUS COLLEGE REP MEETING

COLLEGE REPRESENTATIVE

Name:

Telephone Number:

Email:

Date/time:

Location:

Notable information:

Is there any additional information you would like to request?

Remember that thank-you note!

OFF-CAMPUS COLLEGE REP MEETING

COLLEGE REPRESENTATIVE

Name:

Telephone Number:

Email:

Date/time:

Location:

Notable information:

Is there any additional information you would like to request?

Remember that thank-you note!

OFF-CAMPUS COLLEGE REP MEETING

COLLEGE REPRESENTATIVE

Name:

Telephone Number:

Email:

Date/time:

Location:

Notable information:

Is there any additional information you would like to request?

Remember that thank-you note!

OFF-CAMPUS COLLEGE REP MEETING

Name of School:

COLLEGE REPRESENTATIVE

Name:

Telephone Number:

Email:

Date/time:

Location:

Notable information:

Is there any additional information you would like to request?

Remember that thank-you note!

OFF-CAMPUS COLLEGE REP MEETING

Name of School:

COLLEGE REPRESENTATIVE

Name:

Telephone Number:

Email:

Date/time:

Location:

Notable information:

Is there any additional information you would like to request?

Remember that thank-you note!

OFF-CAMPUS COLLEGE REP MEETING

COLLEGE REPRESENTATIVE

Name:

Telephone Number:

Email:

Date/time:

Location:

Notable information:

Is there any additional information you would like to request?

Remember that thank-you note!

OFF-CAMPUS COLLEGE REP MEETING

Name of School:

COLLEGE REPRESENTATIVE

Name:

Telephone Number:

Email:

Date/time:

Location:

Notable information:

Is there any additional information you would like to request?

Remember that thank-you note!

OFF-CAMPUS COLLEGE REP MEETING

COLLEGE REPRESENTATIVE

Name:

Telephone Number:

Email:

Date/time:

Location:

Notable information:

Is there any additional information you would like to request?

Remember that thank-you note!

OFF-CAMPUS COLLEGE REP MEETING

COLLEGE REPRESENTATIVE

Name:

Telephone Number:

Email:

Date/time:

Location:

Notable information:

Is there any additional information you would like to request?

Remember that thank-you note!

OFF-CAMPUS COLLEGE REP MEETING

COLLEGE REPRESENTATIVE

Name:

Telephone Number:

Email:

Date/time:

Location:

Notable information:

Is there any additional information you would like to request?

Remember that thank-you note!

OFF-CAMPUS COLLEGE REP MEETING

COLLEGE REPRESENTATIVE

Name:

Telephone Number:

Email:

Date/time:

Location:

Notable information:

Is there any additional information you would like to request?

Remember that thank-you note!

OFF-CAMPUS COLLEGE REP MEETING

Name of School:

COLLEGE REPRESENTATIVE

Name:

Telephone Number:

Email:

Date/time:

Location:

Notable information:

Is there any additional information you would like to request?

Remember that thank-you note!

OFF-CAMPUS COLLEGE REP MEETING

COLLEGE REPRESENTATIVE

Name:

Telephone Number:

Email:

Date/time:

Location:

Notable information:

Is there any additional information you would like to request?

Remember that thank-you note!

OFF-CAMPUS COLLEGE REP MEETING

COLLEGE REPRESENTATIVE

Name:

Telephone Number:

Email:

Date/time:

Location:

Notable information:

Is there any additional information you would like to request?

Remember that thank-you note!

ALUMNI INTERVIEW

Name of School:

ALUMNI INTERVIEWER

Name:

Address:

Telephone Number:

Email:

Date/time:

Location:

Notable information:

Did you send a thank-you note? Remember to enter the note in your **Correspondence Journal**

ALUMNI INTERVIEW

Name of School:

ALUMNI INTERVIEWER

Name:

Address:

Telephone Number:

Email:

Date/time:

Location:

Notable information:

Did you send a thank-you note? Remember to enter the note in your **Correspondence Journal.**

ALUMNI INTERVIEW

ALUMNI INTERVIEWER

Name:

Address:

Telephone Number:

Email:

Date/time:

Location:

Notable information:

Did you send a thank-you note? Remember to enter the note in your **Correspondence Journal**.

ALUMNI INTERVIEW

Name of School:

ALUMNI INTERVIEWER

Name:

Address:

Telephone Number:

Email:

Date/time:

Location:

Notable information:

Did you send a thank-you note? Remember to enter the note in your **Correspondence Journal.**

ALUMNI INTERVIEW

ALUMNI INTERVIEWER

Name:

Address:

Telephone Number:

Email:

Date/time:

Location:

Notable information:

Did you send a thank-you note? Remember to enter the note in your *Correspondence Journal.*

ALUMNI INTERVIEW

Name of School:

ALUMNI INTERVIEWER

Name:

Address:

Telephone Number:

Email:

Date/time:

Location:

Notable information:

Did you send a thank-you note? Remember to enter the note in your Correspondence Journal.

ALUMNI INTERVIEW

ALUMNI INTERVIEWER

Name:

Address:

Telephone Number:

Email:

Date/time:

Location:

Notable information:

Did you send a thank-you note? Remember to enter the note in your **Correspondence Journal.**

ALUMNI INTERVIEW

Name of School:

ALUMNI INTERVIEWER

Name:

Address:

Telephone Number:

Email:

Date/time:

Location:

Notable information:

Did you send a thank-you note? Remember to enter the note in your **Correspondence Journal**.

ALUMNI INTERVIEW

Name of School:

ALUMNI INTERVIEWER

Name:

Address:

Telephone Number:

Email:

Date/time:

Location:

Notable information:

Did you send a thank-you note? Remember to enter the note in your **Correspondence Journal.**

ALUMNI INTERVIEW

Name of School:

ALUMNI INTERVIEWER

Name:

Address:

Telephone Number:

Email:

Date/time:

Location:

Notable information:

Did you send a thank-you note? Remember to enter the note in your **Correspondence Journal**.

ALUMNI INTERVIEW

Name of School:

ALUMNI INTERVIEWER

Name:

Address:

Telephone Number:

Email:

Date/time:

Location:

Notable information:

Did you send a thank-you note? Remember to enter the note in your **Correspondence Journal**.

ALUMNI INTERVIEW

ALUMNI INTERVIEWER

Name:

Address:

Telephone Number:

Email:

Date/time:

Location:

Notable information:

Did you send a thank-you note? Remember to enter the note in your **Correspondence Journal.**

ALUMNI INTERVIEW

ALUMNI INTERVIEWER

Name:

Address:

Telephone Number:

Email:

Date/time:

Location:

Notable information:

Did you send a thank-you note? Remember to enter the note in your **Correspondence Journal.**

ALUMNI INTERVIEW

Name of School:

ALUMNI INTERVIEWER

Name:

Address:

Telephone Number:

Email:

Date/time:

Location:

Notable information:

Did you send a thank-you note? Remember to enter the note in your Correspondence Journal.

ALUMNI INTERVIEW

Name of School:

ALUMNI INTERVIEWER

Name:

Address:

Telephone Number:

Email:

Date/time:

Location:

Notable information:

Did you send a thank-you note? Remember to enter the note in your **Correspondence Journal.**

CORRESPONDENCE JOURNAL

Name of School:

DATE	TYPE*	CONTACT NAME	REGARDING

*Type of correspondence: email, letter, fax, telephone call

CORRESPONDENCE JOURNAL

Name of School:

DATE	TYPE*	CONTACT NAME	REGARDING

*Type of correspondence: email, letter, fax, telephone call

CORRESPONDENCE JOURNAL

Name of School:

DATE	TYPE*	CONTACT NAME	REGARDING

*Type of correspondence: email, letter, fax, telephone call

CORRESPONDENCE JOURNAL

Name of School:

DATE	TYPE*	CONTACT NAME	REGARDING

*Type of correspondence: email, letter, fax, telephone call

CORRESPONDENCE JOURNAL

Name of School:

DATE	TYPE*	CONTACT NAME	REGARDING

*Type of correspondence: email, letter, fax, telephone call

CORRESPONDENCE JOURNAL

Name of School:

DATE	TYPE*	CONTACT NAME	REGARDING

*Type of correspondence: email, letter, fax, telephone call

CORRESPONDENCE JOURNAL

Name of School:

DATE	TYPE*	CONTACT NAME	REGARDING

*Type of correspondence: email, letter, fax, telephone call

CORRESPONDENCE JOURNAL

Name of School:

DATE	TYPE*	CONTACT NAME	REGARDING

*Type of correspondence: email, letter, fax, telephone call

CORRESPONDENCE JOURNAL

Name of School:

DATE	TYPE*	CONTACT NAME	REGARDING

*Type of correspondence: email, letter, fax, telephone call

CORRESPONDENCE JOURNAL

Name of School:

DATE	TYPE*	CONTACT NAME	REGARDING

*Type of correspondence: email, letter, fax, telephone call

CORRESPONDENCE JOURNAL

Name of School:

DATE	TYPE*	CONTACT NAME	REGARDING

*Type of correspondence: email, letter, fax, telephone call

CORRESPONDENCE JOURNAL

Name of School:

DATE	TYPE*	CONTACT NAME	REGARDING

*Type of correspondence: email, letter, fax, telephone call

CORRESPONDENCE JOURNAL

Name of School:

DATE	TYPE*	CONTACT NAME	REGARDING

*Type of correspondence: email, letter, fax, telephone call

CORRESPONDENCE JOURNAL

Name of School:

DATE	TYPE*	CONTACT NAME	REGARDING

*Type of correspondence: email, letter, fax, telephone call

CORRESPONDENCE JOURNAL

Name of School:

DATE	TYPE*	CONTACT NAME	REGARDING

*Type of correspondence: email, letter, fax, telephone call

DEFINE YOUR CHOICES: YOU'RE READY TO APPLY!

Now you have a list of schools and you're ready to apply. This is the one component of your application process that you actually *can* control. Accurate execution of each step required to complete the application ensures your file *will* definitely be reviewed by the admissions committee. Your application should reflect your best efforts.

> Please read and reread your Common App and essays and then ask a parent, teacher, or friend to read through them as well. Use the "print preview" feature of the Common App to proofread your entire application before pressing the "submit" button.

"The reality is that we do expect students to follow our application instructions with great detail."

–SHAWN ABBOTT, Assistant Vice President for Admissions, New York University

"Check your spelling!!!"

–PAUL W. HORGAN, Director of College Counseling, Cape Henry Collegiate School, Virginia Beach, Virginia

There is an enormous amount of information to manage while meeting numerous deadlines. Time spent now will save you time (and potential panic attacks) in the future.

"Students and families need to read the fine print, not assume anything! Even among similar institutions there will be different deadlines, requirements, etc."

–NANCY HARGRAVE MEISLAHN , Dean of Admission and Financial Aid, Wesleyan University

It's your responsibility to confirm your file is complete. Not all schools send correspondence requesting missing information. Follow up by phone, check the online service your high school uses, or consult the online tracking system many colleges assign to applicants in order to confirm your application materials have been received.

My daughter's friend submitted an application to a school that reviews them on a rolling basis, hoping to receive an early answer. Months passed until she learned her teacher recommendations had never been received, delaying her application's review.

"The CMC Admission Office has an application portal where applicants can confirm the application credentials our office has received and what items are lacking. The portal lists required application materials only and will not indicate, for example, if we have received an art or an athletic supplement."

—JENNIFER SANDOVAL-DANCS, Director of Admission, Claremont McKenna College

"Just keep in mind that, just as you have the option of contacting us via phone or email, our counselors will be trying to reach you through both media as well. Be sure to check your email and voicemail regularly for important messages throughout the application process."

—JIM ROGERS, Dean of Admission, Marymount Manhattan College

In this section, we walk you through **Folder Set-Up**, which is critical to staying organized. The **Go-To Info** sheet will spare you countless hours of tedious, redundant work. Mailing labels, although optional, give your application a polished look.

Labels are also helpful for those of us with messy handwriting.

FOLDER SET-UP

There is a tremendous amount of information to track in the application process, but this system assures your ability to quickly and accurately meet deadlines, monitor your applications, and respond to further requests for information to support your applications.

Now is the time to take out the 13 folders we suggested you buy.

Label each folder as follows:

Ten School Folders—Assign one folder to each school application by writing the name of the school on the folder tab. Fill each school folder with the following:

- **School Search** form
- **On-Campus Interview** form
- **Off-Campus College Rep Meeting** form
- **Alumni Interview** form
- **Correspondence Log** form
- Copy of school application or supplement, if required
- Copy of the Common App/Universal College Application if you have completed a different version for this school

One Common Application/Universal College Application Folder—Include in this folder:

- Copy of the completed Common App/Universal College Application, with essays

One General Folder—Fill this folder with:

- Testing admission tickets
- Score reports
- Transcript
- Writing samples

One Financial Aid/Scholarship Folder (optional)—Included in this folder are the following:

- Copy of the FAFSA
- Copy of the CSS/Financial Aid PROFILE
- Copy of any other submitted forms and corresponding essays

Always save your work on your data storage device!

GO-TO INFO

You are going to be asked to fill in specific information repeatedly for each application. In order to avoid searching through websites or brochures over and over again, save yourself time by filling in the **Go-To Info** sheet once.

Fill in the **Go-To Info** sheet, making a copy for each school you are applying to. Then, attach each completed sheet to the folder for that school.

The **Go-To Info** sheet includes:

- **Admissions Office mailing address**—Copy this exactly as it appears on the school's website or in its brochure.

"If something is not addressed correctly but goes to another area of the university, there is a high likelihood that it will get back to us, but there are no guarantees."

–SUNIL SAMUEL, Director of Admission, Hofstra University

- **User Name and Password**—User name and password you have been assigned for that particular school's online application.
- **School Codes**—Find each school's SAT and ACT code—usually listed on the application or admissions website—and fill in the space provided.
- **Application Type**—If the school accepts the Common App/Universal College Application and/or requires a supplement, indicate that here.
- **Important Deadlines**—Fill in each school's Early Action, Early Decision, Early Decision II, Regular Decision, and Rolling Admissions application deadlines. If you are submitting supplemental materials and/or applying for individual school scholarships, note the due dates in the spaces provided. Be aware, these due dates may differ from the application due date.
- **Admissions Contact Information**—Note the name, address, telephone number, and email address of your Admissions Office representative.
- **Financial Aid Information**—For each school, fill in the FAFSA code, CSS/Financial Aid PROFILE code, and the corresponding due dates. Use the extra space provided to jot down codes for additional sources of financial aid.

GO-TO INFO

SCHOOL NAME

_____

Your User Name_____

Your Password _____

Admission Office Mailing Address

_____

SCHOOL CODES

College Board_____ ACT_____

APPLICATION TYPE

Common App_____ Supplement_____

Universal College App_____ Supplement _____

School application_____

IMPORTANT DEADLINES

Early Action_____ Early Decision_____ Early Decision II _____

Regular Decision _____ Rolling Admissions _____

School Scholarship_____ Supplemental Materials_____

Admissions Contact Information

Name:

Telephone:

Email:

FINANCIAL AID INFO

FAFSA Code _____ Due Date _____

CSS/PROFILE Code _____ Due Date _____

OTHER Code _____ Due Date _____

OTHER Code _____ Due Date _____

MAILING

We recommend you purchase the following:

- **Mailing Labels:** 2″ × 4″ labels for your printer are the optimal size so that you can fit the full school name and admissions address. Labels can be used for correspondence such as non-electronic applications, supplemental material, and letters providing new information in support of your application.

    Labels can be affixed to pre-addressed envelopes you will give to your high school guidance department, and to teachers and anyone else writing letters of recommendation. Refer to your **Go-To Info** sheet for the correct admissions name and address information.

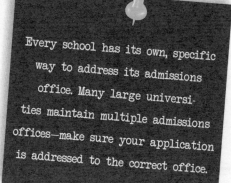

Every school has its own, specific way to address its admissions office. Many large universities maintain multiple admissions offices—make sure your application is addressed to the correct office.

- **Address labels**: 1″ × 2 5/8″ address labels can be used for return address information. Materials submitted by guidance counselors and teachers should include their name and school address on the return address label. Letters of recommendation from outside sources should include their name and work address on the return address label.

You may want to consider using 8 1/2″ x 11″ envelopes when mailing several pages at once. Your pages will look much neater when the admissions officer pulls your unfolded documents out of a large, flat envelope.

CHAPTER 6

PAYING THE BILLS: SHOW ME THE MONEY!

You and your family may have already discussed how you will pay for college. Although your list should include schools within your family's budget, in most cases the cost to attend will require at least some financial aid. Applying to both financial target and reach schools keeps your options open until you have all your admissions decisions and aid packages in hand.

"If you want to go to college this fall, you absolutely can afford to go to college! The key is for students to stay open-minded about the thousands of colleges and universities that exist in the United States today; ranging from elite, high-priced private institutions to larger, public, low-priced community colleges. There isn't just one college out there for each student. There are hundreds. So every student can get admitted to college and every student can afford to go to college."

–JACQUELYN NEALON, ED.D., Vice President,
Enrollment, Communications and Marketing, New York Institute of Technology

---

At first, the financial aid process may seem overwhelming, but the more you understand about the system, the more successful you will be in gaining aid.

There are three types of financial aid:

1. Loans
   a. Need-based loans: Perkins and Stafford are both need-based, federally subsidized loans. Colleges' own loans are also need-based.
   b. Non-need-based loans: Unsubsidized Stafford, PLUS (Parent Loan for Undergraduate Students), and state loans are not need-based.

2. Gift aid is almost always tax-free and never has to be repaid. Included in this list are:
   a. Scholarships: May be need or merit-based.
   b. Grants: School grants may be need or merit-based; state grants are based on need.
   c. Tuition waivers

3. Federal work/study: Students are given part-time jobs, usually on campus to help meet the family's remaining need.

"Do not throw a school off your list just because the price may seem out of your range. You do not know what their scholarship structure is."

—SUNIL SAMUEL, Director of Admission, Hofstra University

Schools require any number of forms in order to apply for financial aid. Check each individual school's website or application, determine which forms are required, and note their respective deadlines. The most commonly required forms are **FAFSA**, **CSS/Financial Aid PROFILE**, and **state and individual school forms**. Helpful websites include www.finaid.org and www.studentaid.ed.gov.

FREE APPLICATION FOR FEDERAL STUDENT AID (FAFSA)

Students must complete a FAFSA application to be considered for all need-based and non-need-based federal and state aid programs and gift aid. FAFSA required programs include:

- **Pell Grant**, which is need-based and primarily for low-income families. You automatically apply for the Pell when you fill out the FAFSA.
- **Federal Academic Competitiveness Grant (ACG)**, a Federal grant program based on both academic performance and need.
- **Federal Supplemental Educational Opportunity Grant (FSEOG)**, which is administered by the colleges themselves at their discretion.
- **National SMART Grant**, which is restricted to third- and fourth-year college students who meet criteria set forth by the Department of Education.
- Loans including the **Perkins loan**, **Stafford loan**, and **PLUS**.

The FAFSA can be completed online at www.fafsa.ed.gov. A PIN is required to complete the online FAFSA. Apply for a PIN at www.pin.ed.gov. Parents should also apply for a PIN to use as their signature for the online FAFSA. Don't forget to jot down your PINs on the **Student's Personal Information** form. FAFSA forms are also available by calling 800-1-FED-AID.

When you submit your FAFSA online, be sure to print out the confirmation page and file it in your **Financial Aid/Scholarship** folder. File a copy if you are submitting by mail, as you are required to send the original. A few weeks after submitting your FAFSA, you will receive a Student Aid Report or SAR. If you filed online, you may retrieve your SAR electronically by using your student PIN. If you have not received a SAR report within four weeks of submitting, call 800-433-3243 or 319-337-5665. File a hard copy of your SAR in your **Financial Aid/Scholarship** folder, as you may need to supply this to the college you attend.

FAFSA errors can cause delays in processing. The later your application is reviewed, the less money there may be available.

Deadlines for the FAFSA differ from school to school. Note the priority and closing filing deadlines on the **Financial Aid Worksheet**. The FAFSA may not be filed until after January 1 of your senior year.

CSS/FINANCIAL AID PROFILE

The CSS/PROFILE form helps schools determine eligibility for non-federal student aid funds. The CSS/PROFILE must be completed online at www.collegeboard.com in order for a student to be considered for all need-based university grants and scholarships. You must register with the College Board in order to complete the CSS/PROFILE. Submit your application and then print the acknowledgment. The acknowledgment includes the data you entered on your application and the list of colleges you've chosen to send your financial aid information to. File this acknowledgment in your **Financial Aid/Scholarship** folder. You may be asked to provide this to the school you choose to attend.

The CSS/PROFILE may be submitted once you have completed your online registration. Before you tackle the actual aid application, review and jot down the priority and closing filing dates on the **Financial Aid Worksheet** provided. Some aid is granted on a first-come, first-served basis; apply as early as allowed. If you submit a CSS/PROFILE form, you will receive an Acknowledgment/Data Confirmation Report from the College Board.

BOUND TO ORGANIZE WORKSHEETS

The **First Things First** form helps you complete the online applications quickly and accurately. To move the process along efficiently, first gather the information required to complete the **First Things First** form. Then go to www.fafsa.gov and print and fill in the FAFSA on the Web Worksheet prior to completing the application. If schools require the CSS/PROFILE, go to www.profileonline.collegeboard.com, print and complete the preapplication worksheet and application instructions prior to working on the online CSS/PROFILE application.

The **Financial Aid Worksheet** will help you with the challenging task of managing deadlines. In the financial aid world, applications have different deadlines, and deadlines are absolute. There are no second chances. The key is to apply as early as possible, stay ahead of deadlines, and respond quickly.

FAFSA and CSS/PROFILE submit your aid applications directly to schools you identify on your applications. FAFSA's six-digit codes and CSS/PROFILE's four-digit codes are available on school websites and on the FAFSA and CSS/PROFILE online sites. Space is provided in the worksheet for you to note the codes relevant to your applications.

> "Families are often very focused on the application process and can forget about deadlines for the financial aid process. Late applications for financial aid are a huge mistake and cost families money in lost scholarships."
>
> —AMY BAUMGARTEL SINGER, Director of College Counseling, The Wheeler School, Providence, Rhode Island

Some colleges or scholarship programs may request you provide additional documents through the College Board's Institutional Documentation Service (IDOC). You will be sent notification from the College Board if such information is needed.

A **Scholarship Log** is provided to help you keep track of available scholarships and important dates. Scholarships are available from individual colleges and universities as well as from private and public sources. A helpful resource to match you with scholarships is www.fastweb.com.

"We have a scholarship consideration deadline of December 1, in advance of our regular decision deadline of January 2. All applicants should note this deadline if they want to be considered for scholarships."

–JENNIFER SANDOVAL-DANCS, Director of Admission, Claremont McKenna College

---

Use the **Comparing Aid Packages** form to determine which packages are best for you. When completing this form, remember that "total cost" equals the sum of tuition and fees, room and board, personal expenses, books and supplies, and travel. Note the notification dates and reply-by dates for individual schools.

You do not want to lose out on an aid opportunity because you missed a response deadline.

First Things First

PERSONAL INFORMATION

Student's Social Security Number:_____

Student's Driver's License Number and State:_____

Alien Registration Number (if you are not a U.S. citizen):_____

PARENT INFORMATION

Mother's (Stepmother's) Social Security Number:_____

Date of Birth:_____

Father's (Stepfather's) Social Security Number:_____

Date of Birth:_____

Date parents became legal residents:_____

Date parents were married, separated, divorced, or widowed:_____

HAVE HANDY

√ Tax returns, W2's, or pay stubs for the past 2 years

√ Bank statements

√ Retirement account information

√ Records of:

Untaxed income (welfare benefits, Social Security benefits, child support)

Veteran's benefits

Investments

Mortgage information

Financial Aid Worksheet

SCHOOL					
FAFSA					
Code					
Priority Filing Deadline					
Closing Deadline					
Date Sent					
CSS/PROFILE					
Code					
Priority Filing Deadline					
Closing Deadline					
Date Sent					
STATE FORMS					
Deadline					
Date Sent					
SCHOOL FORMS					
Deadline					
Date Sent					
OTHER FORM(S)					
Deadline					
Date Sent					
FINANCIAL AID CONTACT					
Name					
Telephone					
Email					

Financial Aid Worksheet

SCHOOL					
FAFSA					
Code					
Priority Filing Deadline					
Closing Deadline					
Date Sent					
CSS/PROFILE					
Code					
Priority Filing Deadline					
Closing Deadline					
Date Sent					
STATE FORMS					
Deadline					
Date Sent					
SCHOOL FORMS					
Deadline					
Date Sent					
OTHER FORM(S)					
Deadline					
Date Sent					
FINANCIAL AID CONTACT					
Name					
Telephone					
Email					

Scholarship Log

NAME OF SCHOLARSHIP	DUE DATE	DATE SUBMITTED

Comparing Aid Packages

SCHOOL					
TOTAL COST					
FAMILY CONTRIBUTION					
GRANTS & SCHOLARSHIPS					
Federal					
State					
College					
SCHOLARSHIPS					
1.					
2.					
TOTAL GRANTS/ SCHOLARSHIPS					
LOANS					
Perkins					
Federal Subsidized					
Federal Unsubsidized					
PLUS					
Other					
TOTAL LOANS					
WORK-STUDY					
VALUE OF AID PACKAGE					
FAMILY OUT-OF-POCKET					
REPLY DATE					

Comparing Aid Packages

SCHOOL					
TOTAL COST					
FAMILY CONTRIBUTION					
GRANTS & SCHOLARSHIPS					
Federal					
State					
College					
SCHOLARSHIPS					
1.					
2.					
TOTAL GRANTS/ SCHOLARSHIPS					
LOANS					
Perkins					
Federal Subsidized					
Federal Unsubsidized					
PLUS					
Other					
TOTAL LOANS					
WORK-STUDY					
VALUE OF AID PACKAGE					
FAMILY OUT-OF-POCKET					
REPLY DATE					

CHAPTER 7

THE HOME STRETCH: YOU'RE ALMOST DONE!

You have submitted your applications and you're almost done! While you await decisions, confirm that all your application materials have been received. Use the **I Did My Job!** checklist during the follow-up stage of your application process. The **Am I In?** and the **Should I/Shouldn't I?** charts will help you sort through your acceptances and choose the college that's best for you. Continue to check your email and "snail mail."

Jack M. didn't check his email account daily and as a result missed the opportunity to participate in a special program offering him generous financial assistance.

"Keeping tabs on letters and emails, tracking deadlines, and scheduling tasks is essential for success."

–LAURA A. BRUNO, Associate Director of Admissions, York College, The City University of New York

---

I DID MY JOB!

As you submit your applications, check off that each application component has been sent to that school. Later, verify either online or by phone that each component has been received by the college or university. Record this information on the checklist as well.

"This is your process—take ownership and follow up with your colleges. Pay attention to deadlines."

–MARIA LAPINS, Senior Assistant Director of Admission, University of Richmond

---

AM I IN?

Congratulations, your job is complete! Should you have any new achievement, share it with your admissions officers.

"Students can always feel free to submit additional materials and updates to their file after completion. Students are welcome to continue to update their application, even after our deadline."

–NICOLE KELMAN, Assistant Director of Admission, Muhlenberg College

---

As you await final decisions, remember both acceptance and waitlist decisions require a response. All schools maintain their own deadlines for a reply to acceptance and waitlist outcomes. Acceptance requires a decision and deposit by a specific deadline to secure your spot in the incoming class. Waitlist outcomes require a response by a stated deadline in order to secure a spot on future consideration lists.

After being waitlisted, you may want to get in touch with an admissions officer to express your interest in attending and to find out if there is any additional information you can provide. You may also consider referring back to your **Correspondence Journal** to reach out to contacts you made at the school earlier in the process.

"There is no greater feeling than receiving your first college acceptance letter. Celebrate your acceptance. You have worked your entire secondary education to achieve this success and regardless of what school the letter comes from, celebrate that milestone, because you only get ONE first college acceptance letter!"

–KEVIN O'SULLIVAN, Director of Undergraduate Admissions, Manhattanville College

---

To ensure your place is guaranteed, please respond on time. A missed deadline is a missed opportunity!

SHOULD I/SHOULDN'T I?

Are you considering more than one of your acceptances? Now is the time to revisit your *Getting Acquainted* forms to complete the **Should I/Shouldn't I?** chart you will find in this chapter. Identify the criteria most important to you and list them under the name of the school you're considering. Does one school have an academic program you are particularly interested in? Consider size, location, and campus personality. If financial aid is relevant, is the school's aid package adequate? Does one school have the Greek life or school spirit you are looking for? Do you feel like you belong as a member of the school community? Pick the things most important to you and compare them from one school you are considering to another.

> **"If a school meets the basic parameters of what you are looking for, go with your gut. If you step onto a campus and can see yourself there for the next four years don't discount that feeling in the final selection process."**
>
> —ED CONNOR, Dean of Admissions, Worcester Polytechnic Institute

We applaud your efforts. You've come a long way and maybe even learned a few new things about yourself in the process. Feel confident you've maintained control of your college application process and have worked diligently toward your goal. You have so much to look forward to.

Good luck!

I DID MY JOB!

SCHOOL NAME	ADMISSIONS TELEPHONE	APPLICATIONS			APPLICATION FEE	SUPPLEMENT	SCORES			
		School	Common App	UCA			ACT	SAT	SAT II	TOEFL

I DID MY JOB!

GUIDANCE		SUPPLEMENTARY MATERIALS	RECOMMENDATIONS			MID-YEAR GRADES	FAFSA	CSS/ PROFILE	DONE!
Transcript	Letter		1	2	3				

AM I IN?

SCHOOL NAME	ACCEPTED		NOT ACCEPTED	DEFERRED	WAITLISTED	
	Response/ Deposit Deadline	Date Mailed			Response Deadline	Date Responded

SHOULD I/ SHOULDN'T I?

CRITERIA	PROS	CONS

ADDITIONAL THOUGHTS:

SHOULD I/ SHOULDN'T I?

Name of School:

CRITERIA	PROS	CONS

ADDITIONAL THOUGHTS:

SHOULD I/ SHOULDN'T I?

CRITERIA	PROS	CONS

ADDITIONAL THOUGHTS:

CHAPTER 8

THE INTERVIEWS

CONVERSATIONS WITH COLLEGE ADMISSIONS OFFICERS

While conducting research for *The College Bound Organizer* we were fortunate to have had the opportunity to interview many college admissions professionals. They were generous in sharing their many insights and experiences with us, and we are confident you will find these conversations invaluable.

Q. How essential is it to coordinate all schedules (standardized testing, college visits, application deadlines...)?

A. During the fall of senior year, demands run high and time is at a premium! Life doesn't stop for the college search and application process. It usually occurs in the context of extraordinarily busy lives marked by school studies, sports, extracurricular activities, and work. It is essential that students get in front of the process and streamline it wherever possible. Having a vision and a "plan of attack" will assist students in maintaining balance while achieving their ultimate goal: acceptance into college!

—LAURA A. BRUNO,
Associate Director of Admissions, York College, The City University of New York

A. I often get asked about mistakes students make or common pitfalls in the process. My response is that students and families need to read the fine print, not assume anything! Even among similar institutions there will be different deadlines, requirements, etc. The process is full of institutional idiosyncrasies and students need to stay on top of it all. A master spreadsheet and/or schedule is essential to success.

—NANCY HARGRAVE MEISLAHN,
Dean of Admission and Financial Aid, Wesleyan University

Q. Which individual components must be in a student's file before you will begin to read the application?

A. Muhlenberg College requires all students to submit an online or paper Common Application, a personal essay, an official high school transcript, a guidance counselor recommendation, two high school teacher recommendations, official SAT and/or ACT scores, and the application fee.

Other non-required, yet highly recommended components are a campus visit and/or interview. If the student has chosen not to submit their SAT/ACT scores for review as a part of our SAT-optional policy, we require an interview with an Admissions Counselor and a graded paper from junior or senior year with the teacher's comments and grade, in lieu of scores.

—NICOLE KELMAN,
Assistant Director of Admission, Muhlenberg College

A. We only read complete applications—transcript, test scores, essay, teacher recommendation, and application fee.

—MARIA LAPINS,
Senior Assistant Director of Admission, University of Richmond

A. All of the required application materials must be in the applicant's file for the file to be flagged as complete and forwarded to the reader except the Midyear Report. We read applications without the Midyear Report. The required components of the freshmen application include: Common Application, Common Application Supplement including analytical essay, Secondary School Report with counselor letter, (2) Academic Teacher Evaluations, Official SAT or ACT scores (we do require the optional writing section of the ACT), Official High School Transcript.

—JENNIFER SANDOVAL-DANCS,
Director of Admission, Claremont McKenna College

Q. When you read an application, what grabs your attention?

A. Since St. Lawrence practices holistic review, I am looking at multiple elements of the application. In terms of the transcript, I am looking to see that the student has challenged him/herself as much as possible within the context of the school's curriculum. I am also looking for evidence of intellectual curiosity, which is often noted in the recommendations from counselors and teachers. However, the item that most often grabs my attention is a well-written essay, which conveys something about the candidate that I might not realize from other parts of the student's file. This is where the candidate can distinguish him/herself as a unique individual.

—ALISON ALMASIAN,
Director of Admissions, St. Lawrence University

A. Every student has a story, so I look for the narrative elements in every document. I can usually find it in essays, even short essays, but there's also a four-year story in the transcript and often good stories in letters of recommendation. I find that knowing something about how a student has changed over time gives me a much better fix on why Rochester would be a great next chapter for him or her.

—JONATHAN BURDICK,
Dean of Admissions and Financial Aid, University of Rochester

A. All schools are looking for the killer scores and top grades. Don't get me wrong, we like them too! That being said, how someone strikes balance in their lives, and the interesting ways in which they get involved outside of the classroom, are what catch my attention. These activities certainly demonstrate that they are an interesting person, and likely to get involved on our campus, but they also show that they are likely to have some balance in their lives and already possess some solid time management skills, which can be critical to success in college.

—ED CONNOR,
Dean of Admissions, Worcester Polytechnic University

A. When reading an application, the primary credential that grabs my attention is the student's transcript. The transcript tells the academic story of the student's four-year performance and oftentimes is the best indicator of the student's ability to be successful at the collegiate level. In addition to looking at the overall performance, I want to see how the student challenged themself at the high school level. Did the student challenge themself with a nice selection of honors and AP courses if their grades indicate that they were capable of performing well in the course? Next, I analyze the standardized test scores if the student chose to submit them. Were the scores consistent with the student's academic performance throughout high school? I also consider the student's I.Q. (Interaction Quotient) or Demonstrated Interest. Has the student demonstrated a desire to be a part of the Manhattanville Community? Did they visit us at a High School Visit or College Fair? Have they visited the campus for a tour or Open House? Did the student interview with a member of our staff? One of my goals as an Admissions Director is to identify students who desire to be a member of the Manhattanville Community. I want Manhattanville to be a first choice school for the students who are applying to the College. In addition, we look at the recommendation letters and college essay.

—KEVIN O'SULLIVAN,
Director of Undergraduate Admissions, Manhattanville College

A. First and foremost, we try to determine if an applicant can succeed academically in our liberal arts curriculum. To that end, we are looking at the student's grades, specifically in his or her "academic" courses, which include math, science, English, history, and foreign language. These subjects are cornerstones of the curriculum here at Marymount, so we want to be sure that each incoming student has a strong foundation in them. Secondly, we are looking at students' SAT or ACT scores for further insight into their level of academic preparedness. Students who demonstrate strong grades and test scores are further rewarded with academic scholarships and admission to our College Honors Program.

A well-written essay also grabs my attention. The essay is your opportunity to show us (not tell us) something about yourself that is not apparent in the rest of your application. You can also show us, by carefully proofreading and editing your essay, that you are taking your Marymount application seriously.

It also catches my attention when a student understands and embodies Marymount's core values. Take the time to learn about the community you are applying to join. The successful Marymount student demonstrates independence, creativity, and ambition. I notice when a student has demonstrated these qualities in his or her previous school setting, by joining clubs, taking on leadership roles, or even speaking up in class. These qualities can shine through in your activities lists, essay, or recommendations.

—JIM ROGERS,

Dean of Admission, Marymount Manhattan College

A. Transcript, SAT Scores, Teacher and Counselor Recommendation, Essay, Extracurricular Activities, Financial Aid: Is the student applying for aid? Be sure to check yes if your family is interested in receiving aid or merit scholarships.

—ZEE SANTIAGO,

Assistant Director of Admissions, Trinity College

Q. Do you welcome email or telephone follow-up questions from applicants? Do you have a preference?

A. Absolutely! Applicants are always welcome to contact the Office of Admissions with questions or concerns. I strongly encourage students to be proactive about the process. While either a telephone call or an email are acceptable, I find email to be slightly more preferable because it creates a history and a record of applicants' inquiries for future reference.

—LAURA A. BRUNO,

Associate Director of Admissions, York College, The City University of New York

A. Definitely. We have four freshman Admission Counselors, two Transfer Admission Counselors, and a Director of International Recruitment who are available to answer questions at any point in the process. (A complete list of Admission representatives and their contact information can be found at www.mmm.edu/become/meet.html.) We welcome questions by either email or telephone, depending on what works best for you. Since high school students tend to be in school during regular business hours, many students find email to be a more practical way of reaching their counselors.

Just keep in mind that, just as you have the option of contacting us via phone or email, our counselors will be trying to reach you through both media as well. Be sure to check your email and voicemail regularly for important messages throughout the application process.

Lastly, I encourage all applicants to take the initiative to contact our office directly, rather than delegating that task to a parent or other family member. It can be tempting to let a parent sit in the driver's seat, especially because you are often very busy in school and because the application process is so overwhelming. While we do appreciate connecting with parents, we always prefer speaking to the student directly. So do not be afraid to reach out to us—we notice and appreciate the gesture.

—JIM ROGERS,
Dean of Admission, Marymount Manhattan College

A. Yes, either is sufficient and an effective way to maintain a relationship with the institution of choice. No, I am accessible either way.

—ZEE SANTIAGO,
Assistant Director of Admissions, Trinity College

Q. Are thank-you letters to Admissions staff and faculty appreciated and noted?

A. Thank-you letters are always appreciated; however, they do not impact the Admission decision.

—LAURA A. BRUNO,
Associate Director of Admissions, York College, The City University of New York

A. Yes! Even at a small school like Marymount, we receive thousands of applications every year. We keep track of all correspondence with students, including thank-you notes, emails, phone calls, visits to the school, and even posts on our Facebook page. By sending a thank-you note, you are demonstrating your organization and interest in Marymount. That conscientiousness does not go unnoticed.

—JIM ROGERS,
Dean of Admission, Marymount Manhattan College

A. Yes, it is greatly appreciated! Aim to maintain consistent communication with the colleges and universities of your choice. Build a relationship with the admissions officer that travels to your region. Set up interviews if possible. Speak with the representative at a fair or when they visit your high school; take their business card, and follow up. Visit, take a tour, and sit in on an information session. Attend Open Houses if they are available. If you cannot visit (i.e., distance), ask for an alumni interview.

—ZEE SANTIAGO,
Assistant Director of Admissions, Trinity College

Q. Do you recommend applicants who have demonstrated a significant commitment to a cocurricular or extracurricular activity support their activities with supplemental materials (i.e., CV, resume, portfolio)?

A. We strongly recommend that applicants follow our application format and complete both the Common Application and the NYU Supplement in their entirety. Students should detail their extracurricular accomplishments on the application, and not expect that we will review a resume instead. For students who are applying to a creative arts program, we do have very specific instructions with regard to the submission of portfolios.

—SHAWN ABBOTT,
Assistant Vice President for Admissions, New York University

A. Resumes are common and should probably go in an application unless the school instructs you not to send one. Keep it to one page; longer resumes look silly—even lazy in a sense, because it doesn't tell us that you've learned how to focus your time and set priorities. I don't think including extra materials ever hurts an application, but I wouldn't encourage a student to spend too much time or put too much stock into this approach unless you're applying for an art, music, etc., major. It's hit-or-miss whether the admissions readers are going to review it, much less appreciate it. Increasingly reading is online, so embedding a link to a webpage with your art or a *brief* video clip of a performance can be effective.

—JONATHAN BURDICK,
Dean of Admissions and Financial Aid, University of Rochester

Q. If a student submits additional supplemental materials in support of his or her application that are not in accordance with your submission requirements, will that material still be considered?

A. The reality is that we do expect students to follow our application instructions with great detail. When an applicant fails to do this—and insists on sending us material not requested— it can potentially damage the impression our readers have of the candidate. We explicitly ask that students refrain from submitting supplementary materials outside of those that are required for our arts programs. Students who ignore this direction can be at a competitive disadvantage in the admission process.

—SHAWN ABBOTT,
Assistant Vice President for Admissions, New York University

A. Overall, I'd say go for it—send it and hope for the best. Yes, you have to allow for the possibility that a college admission office will choose to judge you for not following their rules. However, if the place isn't going to take the time to appreciate who you really are, maybe that's not where you belong anyway.

—JONATHAN BURDICK,
Dean of Admissions and Financial Aid, University of Rochester

A. Students (preferably students, not parents) should always contact admissions offices to see what is appropriate; sending too much of what we do not want may be viewed as a lack of ability to follow directions. If the material is not something an office considers, then in many cases it may be disregarded. Call each college/university to which you plan to apply.

—DARRYL W. JONES,
Senior Associate Director of Admissions, Gettysburg College

Q. Do you often note discrepancies in information between the Common Application and supplemental information submitted? If yes, can you elaborate?

A. Discrepancies of any major type are not common; when we encounter them, we often call college counselors and contact the applicant to get clarity. Honest mistakes are not a problem!

—DARRYL W. JONES,
Senior Associate Director of Admissions, Gettysburg College

A. Discrepancies can come in many different forms. One can be with a student who indicates a very high interest in a club or organization but fails to elaborate on it when submitting other pieces of information. Others can be declaring an interest to be a part of a learning disabilities program and then not going into a bit more detail about how and to what depth they may need services. Other discrepancies may seem minimal but actually cause mass chaos. This can be that addresses, DOB, or SSN do not match what is on a high school transcript.

—SUNIL SAMUEL,
Director of Admission, Hofstra University

Q. Who is responsible for confirming a student's admission file is complete? Does your Admission Office have an online system for students to check whether their standardized scores have been received? If so, are the submitted scores logged in by test date so that students can confirm that all sent scores have been received?

A. The student is solely responsible for confirming their admission file is complete. Muhlenberg College provides every applicant with an identification number and password to check the status of their application online through an ePortal account that the student can create. This account will show the student which credentials we have received and what is still missing. We highly encourage every student to frequently check their status throughout the application process. If the student is unsure if we have received a credential, we encourage the student to contact our office by phone. Many times students think we have received all components because they were mailed to our office, but students should always follow up by checking online or calling our office. Once an application becomes complete, our office will mail a postcard to the student stating that their file is complete and ready for review. Students can always feel free to submit additional materials and updates to their file after completion.

—NICOLE KELMAN,
Assistant Director of Admission, Muhlenberg College

A. We have a staff of six people who track applications, additionally each officer checks all the pieces within an application when he/she opens the file.

—MARIA LAPINS,
Senior Assistant Director of Admission, University of Richmond

A. The CMC Admission Office has an application portal where applicants can confirm the application credentials our office has received and what items are lacking. The portal lists required application materials only and will not indicate, for example, if we have received an art or an athletic supplement. Our application portal simply indicates we have received standardized scores for the applicant, so the only way for an applicant to confirm we received all tests they have requested is to contact our office directly.

—JENNIFER SANDOVAL-DANCS,
Director of Admission, Claremont McKenna College

Q. Once the application deadline has arrived, will you notify candidates of any missing components from their file? Will you allow the students to provide that information at any time past the due date?

A. Muhlenberg will not notify a candidate of any missing components from their file, especially after the deadline has passed. We have very late deadlines for both Regular and Early Decision, so students have ample time to make sure we have received their required components for admission, and we encourage students to check their status online at our admissions ePortal. Students are welcome to continue to update their application, even after our deadline.

—NICOLE KELMAN,
Assistant Director of Admission, Muhlenberg College

A. We notify via BannerWeb. Once a student applies, he/she is given a user name and password to check if credentials are here. We also send emails and letters when the application is incomplete.

—MARIA LAPINS,
Senior Assistant Director of Admission, Richmond University

A. CMC does not typically notify applicants of missing application credentials. We count on the application portal to convey such information to the applicant. We do send out a missing letter and email to applicants in early March if the application is lacking required material.

—JENNIFER SANDOVAL-DANCS,
Director of Admission, Claremont McKenna College

Q. Do applications get lost because they are addressed incorrectly so that the material does not find its way to the Admissions Office properly?

A. If something is not addressed correctly but goes to another area of the university there is a high likelihood that it will get back to us, but there are no guarantees. Since many students are applying online these days and more and more is being done to transmit letters of recommendation, a transcript, etc., electronically, less and less is being lost. This has never been a problem that we have encountered, even though we have an extremely high application volume.

—SUNIL SAMUEL,
Director of Admission, Hofstra University

Q. When reviewing an application are you influenced by any of the following: misspellings, typographical errors, sloppy presentation (i.e., messy handwriting instead of printed labels, overstuffed letter size instead of legal size envelopes)?

A. Many of these issues are not deal breakers, but they may influence the decision process when we assess the students' desirability to attend. If we run into these errors we question if the students are really serious about attending our institution. Misspellings and typos are very bothersome during the essay evaluation and may affect the readers' motivation to continue with reading the essay.

—SUNIL SAMUEL,
Director of Admission, Hofstra University

Q. Are there application missteps you observe repeatedly that you would like to caution future applicants about?

A. Yes! In no particular order…

Think about what your email address may or may not say about you.

Make sure that you are regularly checking the email address you provided to schools. They will be sending important information through that medium.

The correct term is "honor roll," not "honor role."

Have at least two other people read your essay before submitting it. You want to make sure that you are conveying the message you intended as well as make sure that any errors have been corrected. It is extremely difficult to proofread your own work.

Make sure that you have confirmation that your applications are complete. Most schools will alert you when your file is complete. If they do so in writing or by email, keep a record of these contacts. If you have not heard from a school, contact them and then note the date/time of contact and the name of the person with whom you spoke.

—ALISON ALMASIAN,
Director of Admissions, St. Lawrence University

A. I often joke with families that if you were to graph careless essay and application errors against the time of submission you'd see the errors peak around 2 a.m.…if it is that late put it down and take a fresh look at it in the morning. I know everyone is busy, but the application and essay are reflections on you as an individual, and you shouldn't wait to the last minute to complete them. Give the process adequate time. Ask someone to review the application and essay for you. Make sure you are comfortable with them before hitting submit!

—ED CONNOR,
Dean of Admissions, Worcester Polytechnic University

A. Students should avoid relying on spell-check and auto fill-in for essays and supplements. The supplement for Lafayette College should not mention Lehigh University; the act of joining an honors society is an "induction," not an "abduction"…usually proofreading remedies that though.

Students should avoid using essay "banks" for ideas—we scan those to know what the essays are, and plagiarism is something we do not take lightly.

—DARRYL W. JONES,
Senior Associate Director of Admissions, Gettysburg College

A. Our admissions office will often receive phone calls from applicants who say they were unaware that their file was incomplete. It is the student's responsibility to make sure their file is complete. I would also tell students how important it is to demonstrate interest in the college they are applying to, especially if that school is a top choice. Muhlenberg wants to accept students who want to be at Muhlenberg. We will document if a student has interacted with our staff directly through e-mail conversations, phone conversations, campus tours, information sessions, and personal interviews with a staff member. Students should be proactive and take charge. We encourage students to take control of their own college process instead of a parent leading the search. We would love to meet all our applicants in person, if possible.

—NICOLE KELMAN,
Assistant Director of Admission, Muhlenberg College

A. This is your process—take ownership and follow up with your colleges. Pay attention to deadlines.

—MARIA LAPINS,
Senior Assistant Director of Admission, University of Richmond

A. Obviously with the emergence of new technology and advanced "spell check" features, I have noticed an increase in the number of essays that contain some type of error. If you are going to send the same essay to every college, you should at the very least proofread what you send. Every year, there are dozens and dozens of students who write an essay about how much they love Manhattanville College, but then at some point within the essay have a different college's name inserted into the essay!

Oftentimes, I feel as though students feel a need to sign up for 20 different clubs just to show that they were "involved" with a large number of activities in high school. In reality, what I look for when evaluating an applicant is passion. Be passionate about the activities you take part in. You don't need to do a little bit of everything. Rather, put EVERYTHING into the areas about which you are passionate. As a Director, I try to attract and enroll students who can enhance the College environment. I don't want students who have just a little interest in a lot of areas, it creates a bland environment. I want students who have PASSION for what they do and want to bring that PASSION to the College.

—KEVIN O'SULLIVAN,
Director of Undergraduate Admissions, Manhattanville College

A. There are many missteps that can slow down the process, but here are a few:

1. If you are applying electronically, please inform your guidance counselor so they can forward the appropriate high school information.

2. Do not throw a school off your list just because the price may seem out of your range. You do not know what their scholarship structure is.

3. Visit, visit, visit.

4. Be very aware of the application deadlines when researching schools.

5. Ask questions all the time.

—SUNIL SAMUEL,
Director of Admission, Hofstra University

A. We have a scholarship consideration deadline of December 1, in advance of our regular decision deadline of January 2. All applicants should note this deadline if they want to be considered for scholarships. The only additional thing they need to do is indicate "yes" on the Common Application when asked if they want to be considered for merit scholarships. Many times we are contacted by admitted students in April inquiring about scholarships.

Applicants should not hesitate to contact the admission office to confirm we have received their application if they have heard nothing from us and it has been *two weeks* since submitting their application. We send an acknowledgment within two weeks of our receipt of the application to the applicant via email, and we also provide the applicant application portal instructions. Each year there are a handful of applicants who contact our office in April inquiring about their decision and we never received their application.

We require standardized test scores from the College Board or ACT testing agency; we do not accept scores from the high school transcript or self-reported scores.

CMC requires both a personal statement that is part of the Common Application and an analytical essay, which is part of the CMC Supplement; these essays should be different both in writing style and in the content of the essay. Some essays sound very similar and this does not assist us in understanding their different writing styles and viewpoints. If the essays sound too similar they are essentially limiting what we learn from them if they are covering similar topics in both essays.

We require the Common Application and Supplement in order for an application to be complete. There are applicants who submit one without the other, and we cannot access the application from the Common Application unless both applications have been submitted online. If an applicant chooses to mail the application, then both the applications must be mailed.

—JENNIFER SANDOVAL-DANCS,
Director of Admission, Claremont McKenna College

Q. Are there additional comments or anecdotes you would like to share?

A. There is an old saying in college admissions: "The thicker the file, the thicker the student." More is rarely better. Applicants should be effective ambassadors for themselves and must remember their audience: admission counselors are often expected to read between 1,000 and 3,000 applications each year. No admission counselor can read that many applications well if each of those applicants follows his or her own format and submits a bucket of supplementary materials.

—SHAWN ABBOTT,

Assistant Vice President for Admissions, New York University

A. Admissions staff and counselors talk often of the importance of "fit." Each college has a distinct personality, as do the applicants. It is important for students to understand themselves and know what they are seeking from their college experience. Similarly, colleges will seek evidence that an applicant will contribute to their unique community. Both colleges and students have a duty to communicate who they are as effectively as possible to ensure the best possible matches.

—ALISON ALMASIAN,

Director of Admissions, St. Lawrence University

A. Getting organized and staying organized are certainly two of the biggest tasks that high school students face during the process of applying to college. While parents and counselors can assist, the ultimate asset in the college admissions process is a carefully orchestrated plan.

Keeping tabs on letters and emails, tracking deadlines, and scheduling tasks is essential for success. After all, a missed deadline, a forgotten application fee, or a late essay submission can be the difference between a fat acceptance packet and the dreaded rejection letter. Organization maximizes success while minimizing the stress associated with the college application process.

—LAURA A. BRUNO,

Associate Director of Admissions, York College, The City University of New York

A. For the colleges you really want to go to, consider everything listed as "optional" in admissions is actually "mandatory." That's SAT Subject Exams, extra letters of recommendation, invitations to apply for special scholarships or programs, interviews, events in your area, etc. If you literally *can't* complete that extra form or *can't* attend, you can't—but don't *choose* to ignore any opportunity the college admissions office says may be valuable.

It's a fine idea to have an email address that's just for college applications, but if you do, check that email. I see hundreds of high school seniors missing opportunities because they're not in the regular email habit. If one in-box eventually gets too cluttered with email from colleges you've stopped considering, start a new email address and resend that to the smaller number of colleges that are still on your list.

Nothing replaces a campus visit, so seize any opportunity that comes your way to look at college campuses.

The supplements on Common App often mean more to the school's readers than the initial Common App document itself. If you rewrite your main personal statement ten times, don't blow it by submitting a supplement with brief, error-prone, weak short answers on the supplements.

With admissions and aid counselors, after an interview, visit, etc., handwritten thank-you notes work well. Yet this advantage that is relatively easy to gain is often ignored.

—JONATHAN BURDICK,
Dean of Admissions and Financial Aid, University of Rochester

A. The application process can be very stressful and riddled with anxiety-provoking moments, but try and have fun. Visit schools. Get a feel for what they can offer you. In the end, four years goes very quickly when you find the right match, but can go much more slowly if you choose a school for the wrong reasons. If a school meets the basic parameters of what you are looking for, go with your gut. If you step onto a campus and can see yourself there for the next four years, don't discount that feeling in the final selection process. And last but not least, communicate with your parents. You don't want to find out at the eleventh hour that you are on a completely different page than they are!

—ED CONNOR,
Dean of Admissions, Worcester Polytechnic University

A. The admissions process is human, and we look for reasons to admit students, not to deny them. As simple as it may seem, if you are genuine, you always enhance your chances to be admitted if you are academically competitive.

Some things to remember:

1. At a given college or university, there are far more academically competitive applicants than there are places in the entering class, so representing all that you do beyond academics with authenticity is very important.

2. Representing yourself honestly rather than "marketing yourself" will help you to stand out, because too many students try to use the same "devices" based on what they've heard "works" to get admitted.

3. Ask admissions professionals for advice—we enjoy sharing it!

4. Remember to be a student who is an applicant, not an applicant who is a student—you'll enjoy the process more.

—DARRYL W. JONES,
Senior Associate Director of Admissions, Gettysburg College

A. My favorite part about working in college admissions is helping a student and their family through the entire college process from beginning to end, and finding the right match. I know when I meet a great student that is a perfect fit for Muhlenberg. When a student realizes that Muhlenberg is a perfect fit for them in return, that is the best feeling. Seeing that student arrive on campus, flourish as an individual, and graduate is the ultimate goal. My job is to create a bond with a student and help them through the complicated college admissions journey. I also enjoy keeping in contact with students once they arrive and making sure they are receiving the experience on campus they expected. I always hope to convey in words how extraordinary my college experience was at Muhlenberg so that another student will have the opportunity to experience the same.

—NICOLE KELMAN, Assistant Director of Admission, Muhlenberg College

A. My biggest piece of advice to navigating the college search and application process is to take a deep breath! You will often hear through the various forms of media as well as from colleges and high schools about the ultra-competitive admissions standards. However, if you conduct your proper research to find out the academic profiles and requirements of the colleges you are interested in, heed the advice of your school counselors, and take the time to visit the colleges that you are considering, you will most likely find that after the application and admissions process is complete, you will be happy with the results. If you are honest with yourself and honest with the process, you will most likely find out that you end up at the college where you belong! Keep in mind that there are thousands of colleges throughout the United States and a majority of the colleges admit more than 50 percent of the applicants to their college!

One last piece of advice, especially for parents! Be sure to celebrate your (or your son's or daughter's) successes! There is no greater feeling than receiving your first college acceptance letter. In many cases, your first acceptance letter may not be from your first choice college, and that's OK! Celebrate your acceptance. You have worked your entire secondary education to achieve this success and regardless of what school the letter comes from, celebrate that milestone, because you only get ONE first college acceptance letter!

—KEVIN O'SULLIVAN,
Director of Undergraduate Admissions, Manhattanville College

A. The majority of our applicants do a great job of submitting all of the application materials by the deadline, so it can be done. Please do not hesitate to contact the admission office if you do have questions. We would rather handle the questions upfront than deal with them later in the process when it can be more difficult to resolve the problem.

—JENNIFER SANDOVAL-DANCS,
Director of Admission, Claremont McKenna College

CONVERSATIONS ABOUT FINANCIAL AID

Several years ago, we had the opportunity to attend a financial aid seminar featuring Jacquelyn Nealon, Ed.D., Vice President of Enrollment, Communications and Marketing at New York Institute of Technology. We left the presentation with a better understanding of the financial aid process and greater confidence that it could be successfully conquered. We were thrilled when Dr. Nealon recently agreed to speak with us about financial aid.

Q. When discussing the early stages of the college process, you made a profound statement, "everybody can afford to go to college." Can we quote you?

A. Absolutely. I feel 100 percent confident when I look a prospective college student directly in the eye and say, "If you want to go to college this fall, you absolutely can afford to go to college!" The key is for students to stay open-minded about the thousands of colleges and universities that exist in the United States today; ranging from elite, high-priced private institutions to larger, public, low-priced community colleges. There isn't just one college out there for each student. There are hundreds. So every student can get admitted to college and every student can afford to go to college.

Q. What is the most common mistake you see when students apply for financial aid?

A. Missing deadlines, failing to follow through when asked for additional information, and starting the process too late are the most common mistakes that students make when applying for financial aid. The key is to apply as early as possible, stay ahead of deadlines, respond quickly, and not be afraid to ask questions when you are not sure about the process or information you have received.

Q. Do students miss out on aid opportunities because of avoidable mistakes? Can you give us some examples? What is the costliest mistake you see?

A. Students are often so intimidated by the financial aid forms that they misread questions, provide inaccurate/incomplete information, or simply don't apply for aid at all.

The costliest mistake that students can make is to not complete the FAFSA. Every student should take the 30 minutes and complete the simple, easy to follow directions at www.fafsa.gov

gov to file their FAFSA form. Students have nothing to lose by completing the forms and everything to gain.

Even if students end up not qualifying for federal or state grants, understanding what loans are available can be essential to making informed choices. In addition, colleges and universities use the information on the FAFSA form to give out their own institutional monies as well. Without the form on file, they can't even begin to determine if they would like to award additional funds to students.

Q. Do you have an anecdote you would like to add?

A. Over the years, I have counseled hundreds and hundreds of students and their families about how to apply for financial aid, how to choose a college that makes not only good academic sense but also good financial sense, and how to make informed choices. These students have worked so hard for 18 years to build up to this very exciting time in their lives. Their parents have been dreaming of sending their child off to college since the moment the child was born. Their hopes are high, the stakes seem high, and the fear can be debilitating. One of the scariest conversations a parent can think about having with their child is, "I'm so proud of you. You were admitted to all of these terrific schools. But I can't afford to send you to the one you chose."

I like to remind students and their parents to take a deep breath, take a moment to appreciate the amazing accomplishments that have led to this point, compliment the students for committing to continuing their educations by attending college, and then repeat after me: "Where the student goes to college is less significant than the fact that the student GOES TO COLLEGE. The most important factor over a lifetime is having the tools of a college education in your tool belt and knowing how to use them to create a successful career."

CONVERSATIONS WITH HIGH SCHOOL PROFESSIONALS

High school professionals are the front-line advisors. They possess a wealth of information and expertise on the college admissions process.

Q. Please comment on the importance of utilizing the resources of the high school guidance department for students and their parents.

A. The High School Guidance department has a wealth of information for the students and the families. College Admissions representatives often make an outreach to the local high schools for the area they are responsible for reading. These representatives value the relationships developed between the high school counselor and their students. Each year these reps either visit the schools and meet with prospective students and counselors or communicate with them at local venues, over the phone, or through email. The HS Guidance departments are typically the first to be aware of any changes in admission requirements or information that would be relevant to any prospective student.

Additionally, HS counselors work very closely with the actual college applications that students complete—they are an extremely valuable resource when unsure how to proceed with a particular application. Use their expertise—they see hundreds of applications and essays and will be able to offer valuable insight into your responses. This is also true for your student resume and college essays. While we always recommend an English teacher review the essays for grammar, the counselors understand what colleges are looking for with respect to the personal statements and the individual supplements. Again, they see hundreds of essays and have worked with very successful students—please utilize their expertise!

It is imperative that students develop the relationship with their high school counselor.

The student-counselor relationship is critical on so many levels. Counselors are first and foremost trained to assist with many particular areas related to stress, time management, and crisis intervention. Additionally, high school counselors have a specialization in college admissions and the college application process. When students enter ninth grade they often become overwhelmed with the stress of their HS transcript, standardized testing, and college level courses. Students must reach out to the counselor for guidance! As this relationship is cultivated, the counselor is able to assist in carving the path that their students will follow with respect to courses, activities, community service, summer experiences, and finally college selections.

—REBECCA GOTTESMAN,
Assistant Principal, Locust Valley High School

A. It's impossible for any college counselor to know everything about all colleges, but they are great resources for helping families conduct their research and for thinking about the process.

—NANETTE TARBOUNI,
Director, College Counseling, John Burroughs School

Q. Given the fixed number of standardized test dates, how do you guide your students in establishing a schedule and keeping track of this schedule?

A. In our Parent/Student Handbook for Upper School families, we print the list of dates for the ACT and the SAT/SAT Subject Tests for the year for all families to view.

We also have the dates listed on the school's master calendar.

In the early fall of junior year, all parents and students receive a calendar of "Important Dates" for the year that includes our recommendations for test registration for both the ACT and SAT.

As we begin individual meetings with juniors in the winter, we review each student's plan for testing and reaffirm those choices in a "wrap-up" letter that we send to the student along with their initial college list.

Over the summer, we send letters to seniors reminding them of upcoming test dates for the fall.

—AMY BAUMGARTEL SINGER,
Director of College Counseling, The Wheeler School

Q. How do you suggest students get organized and prepare to complete the Common Application?

A. I ask students to write down all the things they spend time doing outside of their academic classes, homework, and sleeping. All of it helps tell the story of who they are and what they might bring to a college community. Once they get this global view of how they spend their time, they can begin to decide which activities carry the greatest importance in their lives and what they want to include on the Common App.

The piece of the Common App that obviously requires the most thought is the personal statement. I like to pose the following question to students as they ponder their topics: "When the admissions committee is sitting at the table choosing between you and other students with the same grades and SAT scores, what do you want them to say about you?" Indeed it is a daunting concept for the average 17-year-old, but forcing them to introspectively consider what is genuinely unique about themselves and what they consider most important for the committee to know is a great exercise. Pragmatically, it also tends to produce the most human, honest, and individualized pieces of writing.

As an exercise, I ask students to write a letter of recommendation for themselves from the perspective of the college counselor. "What would you say?" This is a great essay "brain-stormer" and it can be helpful later when writing the counselor letter of reference in understanding what the student values most about his or her accomplishments.

—PAUL W. HORGAN,
Director of College Counseling, Cape Henry Collegiate School

Q. A student's resume is a snapshot of his or her high school years. Can you tell us how the student can use this resume to highlight his or her accomplishments?

A. Our students are encouraged to put together their resumes through the resume builder function in the Naviance system or use the templates that we share with them in our College Counseling Handbook, which they receive in January of their junior year. However, we do not encourage students to submit these resumes to colleges (unless it is an athletic or special talent resume that a coach or professor might need to see). Students are often asked to report their activities in a particular format prescribed by the colleges themselves. Many colleges permit the use of the Common Application. To help our students prepare for this request we give our juniors a sample of the activities section on the Common Application and ask them to complete that as a rough draft. It is reviewed with their counselor for completeness and then used as a source document for the completion of the actual applications, both the Common Application and other applications, in the fall of their senior year.

—AMY BAUMGARTEL SINGER,
Director of College Counseling, The Wheeler School

A. The resume is exactly that—a way to highlight students' accomplishments! Emphasize students' strengths and leadership first and foremost. Every student has a unique set of strengths and the resume should highlight those as applicable. For example, a strong athlete must highlight all athletic achievements, awards, and leadership first and foremost. Students with research accolades should begin with those. Every resume must be unique to the students' accomplishments.

Make sure you don't overlook the small stuff! Nothing is irrelevant, everything counts!

—REBECCA GOTTESMAN,
Assistant Principal, Locust Valley High School

A. Remember that colleges are not looking for resumes that are a "mile wide and an inch deep." Students should consider highlighting the things into which they have poured the most time and effort, finding the things that have meant the most to them and the things in which they have made the greatest impact. The Common App and most other applications have space for students to fill in their activities. Students should remember to list these "*in their order of importance to you*" as the directions indicate. Students need to understand that college admissions officers are trying to get a sense of the individual by evaluating how that individual has spent his or her time. Being an avid skier or rock climber may tell as much and count as much as listing that you fulfilled 20 hours of a community service requirement at the local shelter.

Students should remember to explain their activities if they are not commonly understood things. For example, in Virginia Beach, the annual "Neptune Festival" selects a court of "Neptune Princesses" from a competitive group of local teens. In reality, this is quite an honor and it carries with it serious community service investment and a year-long commitment. Without the explanation, an admissions reader could misinterpret it as "fluff." At the nearby Suffolk Peanut Festival, they crown a "Peanut Princess"! You get the drift. Explain, explain, explain. But don't be so wordy that it is cumbersome.

—PAUL W. HORGAN,
Director of College Counseling, Cape Henry Collegiate School

Q. The application process does not end once the student submits his or her application. What do you advise the student to do from this point on?

A. Read your email! Colleges communicate primarily through email and expect timely responses. Failure to respond may result in missed opportunities (scholarships, housing, registration for courses). Many times colleges email students an access code or special link for the purpose of tracking their application materials. BE SURE TO CHECK THESE LINKS FREQUENTLY!

One way to stay organized is to keep a list of the schools you applied to next to your computer with each school's user name and password. The user name and password always vary based on the school and it is best to be able to easily access this information. Students often become frustrated when they forget this information and that only delays this process.

Please continue to update your HS counselor. The counselors are often aware of new and additional opportunities that become available. The more you stay in touch with your counselor, the more opportunities you will have. In addition, counselors are often in contact with college representatives and are always happy to provide follow-up information to the colleges their students have applied to.

Most important, if students are deferred or offered a spot on the waitlist, the counselor is the best advocate you have and will reach out to the representative from that particular school to continue to support their student's application!

—REBECCA GOTTESMAN,
Assistant Principal, Locust Valley High School

A.

1. Keep their focus—remain academically engaged.

2. Don't develop senioritis.

3. Continue to think about which college community will serve their growth and development.

—NANETTE TARBOUNI,
Director, College Counseling, John Burroughs School

Q. Are there admissions missteps you observe repeatedly that you would like to caution future college applicants about?

A. Families are often very focused on the application process and can forget about deadlines for the financial aid process. Late applications for financial aid are a huge mistake and cost families money in lost scholarships.

We advise our students to complete their essay over the summer before their senior year. It helps to get what is seen as one of the most torturous parts of the application underway before students have the nightly load of homework, athletic practices, and other commitments added. There are always a few who don't take the advice and end up regretting it later.

Submitting supplementary information to colleges, like art portfolios and musical recordings, can be a confusing process. Refer directly to the institutional websites for directions—one size does not fit all! If in doubt, don't guess; call the college directly.

—AMY BAUMGARTEL SINGER,
Director of College Counseling, The Wheeler School

A. Remember that there are 24 hours in a day. If the total daily hours on your list of activities adds up to more than 24, it calls them all into question.

1. Check your spelling!!!

2. Don't forget to send your scores.

3. Don't have your parents make calls that you can make.

4. Apply to a balanced list of schools.

Remember that the most important school on your list is the one you love, you can afford, and that you know you will get into. When I think of the word "safety" I think of seat belts, air bags, and the little yellow oxygen mask that drops out of the ceiling if the plane is going to crash! We are all glad that these things exist, but do you really want to try them out? Same thing applies to the safety school concept. Find a solid backup option you can live with.

—PAUL W. HORGAN,
Director of College Counseling, Cape Henry Collegiate School

A. Parents can be too involved—students need to do their own work, including the typing.

—NANETTE TARBOUNI,
Director, College Counseling, John Burroughs School

Q. We would appreciate any additional comments or anecdotes you would like to share.

A. We have a panel of our seniors come to an annual junior retreat in the spring and talk about their experiences with the process. Everything from managing deadlines, visiting colleges, writing the essays, and managing the expectations of teachers and parents is discussed. When students hear this information from their peers, it is a powerful way for them to get good information.

Communicate with the teachers who are writing your recommendations early. They spend hours of their own time writing these recommendations and a last-minute ask to a teacher is asking for a "last-minute" effort from a busy teacher. Also, be sure to thank your teacher with a handwritten note—respectful communication goes a long way!

Stay organized! No pun intended with the title of the book, but this is the most surefire way to minimize the stress of the college process.

—AMY BAUMGARTEL SINGER,
Director of College Counseling, The Wheeler School

A. The college application process is an ever-changing process! Every year changes occur with respect to application criteria, modifications to the admissions process, and variations of the deadlines.

The college application process is a progression. Start early and break it up into small, manageable tasks. Most important, utilize all the resources available to you!

—REBECCA GOTTESMAN,
Assistant Principal, Locust Valley High School

A. The college application process is far easier than the process of deciding where to send them. Most of the application is personal information, objective data, and relatively simple answers. The essays can be paralyzing to even the brightest students, but ultimately there is a lot of time and support available to get them done.

My advice for getting into college is to *apply to the right schools.* It may sound overly simplistic, but when a college reader sees a student who fits their institution, that student is most likely to get the benefit of the doubt. If you apply to schools where your academic performance is far below their standards, there isn't really anything you can do in your application to make a positive difference. You are getting a thin envelope. When you apply to a place where your academic record is near the top of their pool of applicants, you have to go to great lengths on the application to blow it. Where the rubber hits the road on apps is at the schools where the giant domino is teetering back and forth. Do a good job and it may fall in your favor. Make careless errors and rush through it, and the domino might fall right back on your head. The point: look for the right fit, both academically and personally, and you are likely to have some great options for life after high school.

—PAUL W. HORGAN,
Director of College Counseling, Cape Henry Collegiate School

ACKNOWLEDGMENTS

The idea for *The College Bound Organizer* was sparked by our own personal experiences with the college admissions process.

We want to thank our agent, Anne Marie O'Farrell, for believing in us. Your experience and guidance set us in the right direction. Your insight paired us with the perfect publisher, Sourcebooks. Thank you to the wonderful team who worked so hard to make this collaboration seamless. Peter Lynch, your passion and knowledge of the college-bound market was invaluable.

We are thankful for the contributions made by two special people. Leslie Guccione, a gentle critic, provided us with just the right amount of thoughtful input. Your overwhelming enthusiasm in the early stages of our project was encouraging. Jane Incao's creativity translated our ideas into a visual reality. Your excitement fueled our determination.

Barbara Kelly Vessa, we are indebted to you on so many levels for your unwavering support. You have worn many hats: great friend, wise legal counsel, and trusted advisor.

Emmy Liss, we are grateful you so graciously offered to serve as our go-to, on-call editorial and technical support team. Your ingenuity, perceptiveness, and endless patience are priceless gifts you shared.

Thank you to the many admissions professionals who generously offered their time and thoughts. We are confident your candid comments and wisdom will be essential to our readers.

This book would never have been possible without our six college-bound students and the lessons we learned on our journeys together. We are so proud of you and your successes.

George and Sam, our proud ambassadors, you made this possible.